Work Comp Playbook
for Employers

The Work Comp Playbook for Employers
A Proven Strategy to Reduce Cost

Stephen P. Heinen, AAI, CWCP
Risk Management Inc.

Alpharetta, GA

Although the author and publisher have made every effort to ensure that the information in this book was correct at the time of first publication, the author and publisher do not assume and hereby disclaim any liability to any party for any loss, damage, or disruption caused by errors or omissions, whether such errors or omissions result from negligence, accident, or any other cause.

Copyright © 2014 by Stephen P. Heinen

All rights reserved. No part of this book may be reproduced or transmitted in any form or by any means, electronic or mechanical, including photocopying, recording, or any information storage and retrieval system, without permission in writing from the publisher. For more information, address BookLogix, c/o Permissions Department, 1264 Old Alpharetta Rd., Alpharetta, GA 30005.

ISBN: 978-1-61005-517-8

10 9 8 7 6 5 4 3 2   081814

Printed in the United States of America

♾This paper meets the requirements of ANSI/NISO Z39.48-1992 (Permanence of Paper)

A portion of the book's proceeds will be donated to Kids' Chance of Georgia, Inc.

The mission of Kids' Chance of Georgia, Inc. is to provide educational scholarships to the children of Georgia workers who have been seriously, catastrophically, or fatally injured in work-related accidents. Kids' Chance of Georgia began reaching out to other states and encouraged and assisted them in establishing their own Kids' Chance organizations. Thanks to their efforts, twenty-five states have organized Kids' Chance programs that are actively providing need-based scholarships to the families of seriously injured workers, and new Kids' Chance organizations are being formed each year. To find out more about the Kids' Chance program in your state, please visit www.kidschance.org.

Table of Contents

Acknowledgments ix
Introduction xi
Chapter 1 **PLOT** 1
Chapter 2 **Process** 3
    Section 2.1 P1 Pre-hire 5
    Section 2.2 P2 Post-offer 17
    Section 2.3 P3 Prevention 27
    Section 2.4 P4 Post-claim 49
Chapter 3 **Loss** 67
    Section 3.1 Total Cost of Risk - TCOR 68
    Section 3.2 Analyzing a Loss Run 74
    Section 3.3 Experience Rating and Classifications 74
    Section 3.4 Claims IQ 79
Chapter 4 **Organization** 89
    Section 4.1 Safety Culture 90
    Section 4.2 Employee Perception Survey 93
    Section 4.3 Safety IQ 97
Chapter 5 **Training** 103
    Section 5.1 Subject 104
    Section 5.2 Method 108
    Section 5.3 Tracking 110
    Section 5.4 Return on Investment (ROI) 112

Chapter 6	**Return to Work: Use of Light Duty Work,** *Greg Presmanes*		115
	Section 6.1	Introduction	115
	Section 6.2	State Statutory Code	116
	Section 6.3	Model Return to Work Practices	125
	Section 6.4	Conclusion	131
Chapter 7	**Coordination of Benefits,** *Joe Chancey and Leigh Lawson Reeves*		**137**
	Section 7.1	Introduction	137
	Section 7.2	Covered Employers	138
	Section 7.3	Covered Employees	140
	Section 7.4	"Disability" vs. "Serious Health Condition"	141
	Section 7.5	Light-Duty Work as a "Reasonable Accommodation"	146
	Section 7.6	Dual Litigation	149
	Section 7.7	Conclusion	149
Chapter 8	**Underwriting**		**151**
	Section 8.1	Underwriter Insights	151
	Section 8.2	NCCI	153
	Section 8.3	Premium Audit	160
Chapter 9	**Resources**		**163**
Conclusion			**173**
Suggested Reading List			**175**
More Resources			**177**

Acknowledgments

It is an honor and a privilege to have an opportunity to acknowledge some of the people who have made this book possible. I have published many books on the topic of workers' compensation but have never published a comprehensive treatise like the one contained in this book. Thanks to the team at BookLogix for their guidance and editorial assistance helping me put my knowledge into practice.

Many of the lessons I teach in this book were passed on to me from people that have had a huge impact on my life. My mom and dad have been a consistent influence in my life and have taught me to never compromise my principles. My high school coach, Billy Ellis, had a huge impact on me. He was a great coach and a better teacher. He strongly encouraged me to get into coaching and was a little disappointed when I chose business school. Cancer took him way too young, but I think he would have been proud of my devotion to teaching.

I have had many great bosses and partners along the way. My first boss out of college was an underwriting manager from the Bronx, Vinnie D, who taught me how to conduct myself in the insurance business. I credit my two years with The Hartford as the place where I laid the foundation for my career and am truly grateful that Jerry Claire took a chance on a country boy from the University of Georgia. When I moved to the agency side of the business, I was fortunate to have Harold Smith and John Williams as mentors. They instilled in me the value of reputation.

A huge amount of credit goes to Orielle Doud, my account manager for over twenty-three years. If it weren't for her stewardship with our clients, I would never have had the time to work on projects like these. I would also like to thank Kathy Oliver for helping me shape my claims IQ.

And a huge shout-out goes to the hundreds of employers, insurers, third party administrators, and other providers that have participated in the Certified Workers' Compensation Professional (CWCP) program I have had the privilege of administering since 1999. Many of the best practices discussed in this book were honed through feedback received by their participation in the CWCP program.

Acknowledgments

I want to recognize my two boys, Hurst and Carson. I have learned that raising children is very similar to managing employees. It is just as tough setting the family culture as it is establishing a company culture. You have to find the right balance of discipline and rewards to motivate them, and most importantly, you have to lead by example. I am very blessed to have two amazing sons and hope that I am instilling the right stuff in them. Finally, I want to thank Tammy. She is more than the love of my life, she is also the ghostwriter behind this book and my sounding board for many ideas and plans. She is the reason this book has become a reality.

I hope you learn something from the book, and if you do, please pass that knowledge along to someone else. One of the lessons I have learned through over thirty years in this industry is that gaining knowledge is not nearly as rewarding as sharing knowledge with someone else. I have devoted a section of my website to your feedback so you can share your thoughts with others at www.managedcomp.net.

Introduction

> Most of what we call management consists of making it difficult for people to get their work done.
>
> – Peter Drucker

To open a meeting with a new prospective client, I will often pose the question, "If safety is first, what is second?" This generally initiates a pretty meaningful dialogue. Obviously, my intent is to challenge them to think beyond the obvious, open their minds to a bigger picture, thus changing their perspective on the status of their current workplace safety program. An accountable and effective workplace safety program does not have to be overwhelming, but it does require *focus* and *commitment*. This book will give you focus and motivate you to have the organizational commitment to implement the programs outlined within its pages.

COMPOINTS

IF SAFETY IS FIRST, WHAT IS SECOND? YOU CANNOT SIMPLY USE SLOGANS AND BANNERS. FOR SAFETY TO TRULY BE FIRST, THE WHOLE ORGANIZATION HAS TO BUY IN.

Introduction

I do a lot of teaching and public speaking and I typically come away from a conference with more knowledge than I probably impart on the groups. That certainly has been the case with the CWCP program. It has been an amazing opportunity to lead this program for the past fifteen years. Imagine over 200 different insurance carriers, self-insured, and third party administrators collectively sharing their best practices. Their diverse strategies have given me a very broad perspective, which has evolved my risk management philosophy. One of the biggest challenges I face is the fact that every organization is different. People learn differently and so do organizations.

Let me backtrack. I graduated from the University of Georgia with a BBA in Risk Management. My first job was with the Hartford Insurance Company, which had one of the industry's leading training programs, so I thought I had a boatload of risk management knowledge. I had my first opportunity to demonstrate "my advanced learning" when I moved back to Georgia and went to work for a local insurance agency. The president of the agency asked me to help him implement a workplace safety program for a large poultry processor he had as a client. I went to work. I followed the textbook education and training I had received. I reviewed OSHA logs and loss runs and toured the operations. I consulted with safety experts. I drafted what I thought was a "best in class" safety program. Then the big day came. The company summoned all the managers and supervisors into a large room and at the head of the table were my boss and the president of the poultry company. I was confident as I passed out my fancy handouts outlining all the new policies and procedures I was going to implement to help this company reduce their workers' comp costs. Once the copies were passed out, I began outlining my plan. My confidence quickly left the building as I saw all the blank stares looking back at me. I lost the group within five minutes. It was a total flop. I think, given my actual lack of real world knowledge, the program was pretty solid. So why did it bomb? The answer has guided me over the last thirty years. I failed to understand the organization's safety culture when I drafted their risk management plan. My program would have gotten an A+ in Risk Management 305, but it did not resonate with anyone in the room. Was it their fault for not understanding my risk management plan OR my fault for not understanding their organization's Safety IQ? I think we all know the answer.

For almost twenty years, my company slogan has been, "We Put Knowledge Into Practice." I have prided myself in giving organizations actionable advice. In fact, I feel so strongly about actionable advice, I am looking to evolve my slogan to something more actionable. Maybe after you read this book you can offer some suggestions.

Workers' compensation is a very challenging process. With the recent economy and changing demographics in the workplace, I would argue that managing a workers' compensation program has never been more difficult.

Introduction

Consider:

- Everybody is having to do more with less. Adjusters have larger caseloads and many companies have reduced their HR and safety staffs. Employees are working longer hours, and perhaps, multiple jobs just to make ends meet. People are worn out. This reduces productivity and increases accidents.

- We have older workers in the workforce. According to BLS (Bureau of Labor Statistics) in 2012, workers over sixty-five had the lowest incidence rate of any age group, but they required the longest time away from work to recover. Workers' Comp pays for worn out workers.[1]

- It is getting increasingly more difficult to get younger employees engaged in having a career. Many view a job as a paycheck until a better opportunity comes along.

- Relationships between organizations and employees are getting weaker, which is why some people believe that company loyalty is dead. Company loyalty (or culture) directly impacts work comp costs.

- According to recent studies, the average employee turnover rate is predicted to rise from 20.6% in 2012 to 23.4% by 2018. This represents 192 million separations.[2]

- According to a recent MetLife Employee Benefits Survey, employee loyalty is at a seven-year low and 76% of the employees surveyed would leave their job if they could.[3]

- Training and compliance needs have increased and so has the diversity of the employees, making training much more difficult.

Keeping employees engaged in their job is a challenge for any employer, and the above referenced factors are making the job even more difficult. If it is tough for an employer to engage an employee, imagine how difficult it is for a third party adjuster! Most employers outsource their claims handling to an insurance carrier or a third party administrator (TPA), or perhaps they outsource to a PEO (Professional Employment Organization). These entities primary responsibility is to manage the payment of claims and coordinate medical treatment, which are both very important activities. But they typically only manage about 30 percent of the workers' comp process. The other 70 percent is managed by the employer. While I will discuss strategies to help you manage your carrier, TPA, or PEO, most of this book is devoted to the 70 percent that falls on your side of the fence.

If you are an employer, please go to www.managedcomp.net and register your book. I realize that I cover a lot of material in the book, but if you register, you will receive some free tools to help you better utilize the information in the book. We limit this offer to employers. If you are an insurance broker, please contact us about *The Work Comp Playbook for Brokers*.

Introduction

This book, as well as the resource information on our website, will be of great help to you, but you probably will need additional assistance to organize and prioritize your effort. Your insurance broker (I use the term agent and broker synonymously) should be your first stop. I have been a risk and insurance advisor, which is a fancy name for an insurance agent/broker, for over thirty years. Most brokers understand that to compete in today's market they have to be more than placement for your insurance. Today's broker should be able to act as your outsourced risk manager. I do a lot of training and can tell you that brokers today are ramping up their consultative skills, and can help you on your risk management and safety plan. We will discuss this in more detail in the chapter on resources, but just know, once you make the commitment to improve your safety culture, your broker will gladly jump at the opportunity to become part of your efforts to improve your workplace safety program.

I spend a lot of time trying to identify opportunities to streamline my clients' policies, procedures, and paperwork. I follow a theory of Stephen Covey that says, "The main thing is to keep the main thing the main thing." With this in mind, and knowing the big "to-do lists" my clients are faced with every day, I created a three-part litmus test that my team uses when developing and implementing any policy or procedure.

1. If it is important, it should do three things. For example, if you want to do a payroll stuffer with a safety message consider having a sign off on the back that asks the employee if they have had a claim in the previous period (since the last payroll stuffer) and not reported it. When the employees drop their signed payroll stuffer back in the box, consider this an entry into your safety motivation program for some small giveaway. One simple payroll stuffer that produced three benefits. You have delivered a safety message, gotten an important compliance sign-off, and provided a positive by using the form as an entry into your safety motivation program.

2. If it is critical, then it should do two things. You will learn about the importance of written job descriptions. They are a critical part of your workplace safety program and should be used in your hiring and return to work process.

3. If the law requires it, then we have to do it. But you can still try and simplify. For example, if you are in an OSHA-regulated industry, you must keep an OSHA 300 log and post a 300A from February 1 through April 30 each year. Many organizations are using claims tracking software that will prepopulate the OSHA logs.

I encourage you to resist the common practice of creating a mountain of policies and procedures. By using the litmus test above, establish your "main thing" and keep it the "main thing," and use the extra time you'll create motivating your employees to work safely, you will see dramatic improvements in your workplace safety!

So let's get started. The next chapter will overview my overall risk management strategy which I call PLOT.

---

[1] "Nonfatal Occupational Injuries and Illnesses Requiring Days Away From Work, 2012," Bureau of Labor Statistics, press release, http://www.bls.gov/news.release/osh2.nr0.htm.

[2] "Are Employees a Flight Risk?," HayGroup website, http://atrium.haygroup.com/uk/your-challenges/misc.aspx?id=3831.

[3] Quoted in "Declining Employee Loyalty: A Casualty of the New Workplace," *Knowledge@Wharton*, blog, http://knowledge.wharton.upenn.edu/article/declining-employee-loyalty-a-casualty-of-the-new-workplace/.

Chapter 1
PLOT

> The rules of navigation never navigated a ship. The rules of architecture never built a house.
>
> – Thomas Reid

Compass has been the central theme to my company since its inception in 1996. There are four points on a compass, and there are four points to my risk management strategy. For centuries, the compass has been a useful tool created to plot a course for travelers to help them safely navigate to a desired destination; therefore, it was very fitting, and symbolic, to call my risk management strategy **PLOT**. The four points to **PLOT** are **P**rocess, **L**oss, **O**rganization, and **T**raining, all designed to help you navigate to an accountable and effective workplace safety process. What makes my risk management approach unique is the holistic approach integrating safety and claims.

My risk management strategy starts with *Process*. I have seen many good risk management efforts fail because all the focus was on policies, procedures, and programs, which may yield compliance, but an effective Process yields results. Understanding the true cost of *Loss*, the second point, is critical to the economic health of any organization. The third point is *Organization*. When I talk about Organization, I am referring to an organization's safety culture. Leading organizations that are committed to providing safe work environments for their employees dedicate the necessary resources to ensure that safety truly is first in their organization. And the final point in the strategy is *Training*. Workplace learning is not rocket science. So why do many organizations fall short? Mostly because organizations do not have a training plan that takes into account all the items discussed in the first three points.

The **PLOT** process combines all of the industry's "best practices" and has delivered proven results. If you implement any of the strategies outlined in this book, be sure to communicate this to your broker, so

PLOT

they can evidence this to the underwriter. This will give your broker ammunition to improve your renewal terms. You will see me refer to the Workers' Comp Scorecard throughout the book. I use my own proprietary scoring process to gauge, monitor, and benchmark my clients' progress, and I use the scoring process to negotiate better terms with the insurance carriers. But you don't have to have a Workers' Comp Scorecard to get better terms. You simply have to evidence your best practices.

Chapter 2
Process

comP4

A safety program may yield compliance, whereas a safety process yields results. Most workplace safety programs I have seen take a "one-size-fits-all" approach. That simply does not work. While many of the basics of a workplace safety program apply to every organization, I have never seen two organizations that are exactly alike. I want to start by saying, as I guide you through the comP4 process you will have to tailor the program to meet your specific needs. The comP4 is the heart of the PLOT strategy, and is the basis for my workers' comp scorecard. In the description of PLOT, I gave you the analogy of four points on a compass. As we discuss comP4, I want you to visualize that each of the four *P*s represents a tire on your automobile. Everybody knows that to get the highest performance from your tries you have to maintain each tire. You don't check the tire pressure on three out of your four tires! The other important point is it doesn't matter which of your tires is flat. When you have a flat, your vehicle is disabled. As I walk you through the comP4 process, some of the aspects of this process will have more importance than others, but you must not lose sight that all four *P*s of the comP4 process are important!

Back in 2000, I was doing some consulting for a broker friend of mine for a large homebuilder. I had to try to commoditize my risk management process by breaking down the steps I went through to analyze a risk. This exercise was the catalyst for comP4. Over the past fourteen years, I have had hundreds of employers utilize this process to improve their workplace safety program. If you successfully implement comP4, the process will evolve and grow, just as your business evolves and grows every day. Please note that the comP4 process is an extremely comprehensive process, but you do not have to implement every step in the process to impact your organization. The fact is few organizations implement every step in the comP4 process. With the assistance of your insurance broker, you can map out which elements of the comP4 process best fit your organization.

So let's jump into the process. The next page contains a flowchart that highlights P1 and P2 of the comP4 process. A copy of this flowchart is contained in our employer outline.

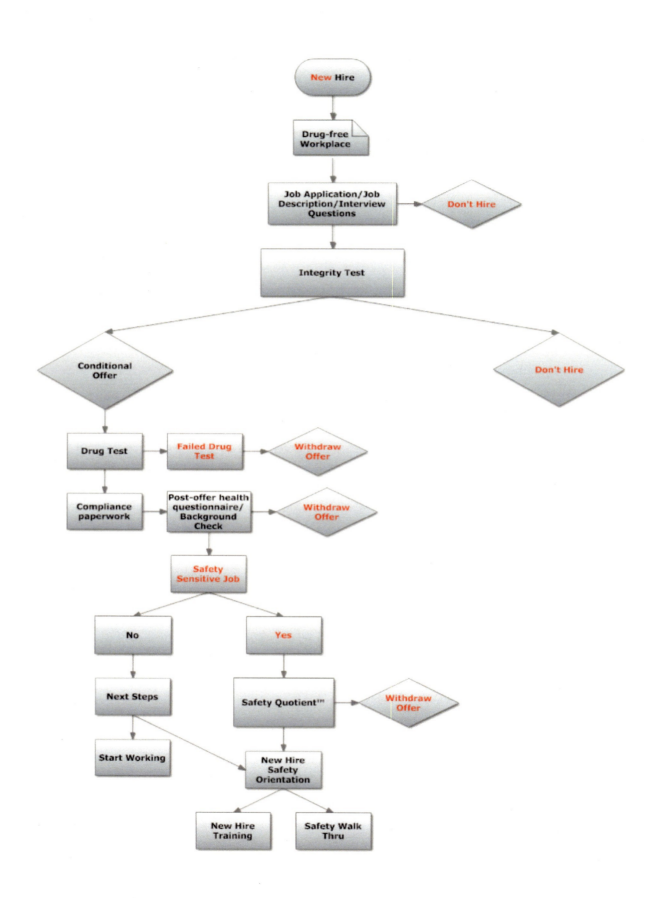

Section 2.1

P1 Pre-hire

C✥MPOINTS

> DID YOU JUST HIRE YOUR NEXT WORK COMP CLAIM? A BAD HIRE IS AN EXPENSIVE HIRE. P1 IS YOUR FIREWALL TO KEEP NEW HIRES FROM INFECTING YOUR SAFETY CULTURE.

Hindsight is 20/20, right? I have heard this thousands of times over my career. When a claim happens, the employer reflects, "Why did we hire that person?" Oftentimes, employers will, for a myriad of reasons, overlook their own best practices to make an expedient hire to fill a position. Then the poor hiring decision manifests into a workers' compensation claim. I often tell my clients that workers' comp is an expensive program to fix hiring mistakes. Why? Because workers' compensation pays income benefits. Yet organizations do it every day! The reason is simple—most organizations do not analyze the cost of bad hires. We will talk more about these costs under the Loss section, but a survey by CareerBuilder showed 41 percent of employers placed the cost of a bad hire over $25,000 while another 25 percent placed the cost over $50,000. The biggest problem most employers have, according to the survey, is the need to hire quickly. A lot of my work is in manufacturing and food processing, so I realize that there are times when an organization simply has to fill positions. But 38 percent of the businesses surveyed stated the need to hire quickly was the cause behind most of the bad hires.[1] A company with 1,000 employees and a 35 percent turnover rate could lose a staggering $8,750,000 per year in bad hiring decisions assuming that the employees being lost are coming into hourly wage positions. The costs climb higher if you factor in salary positions. Decreasing that turnover rate by 50 percent could easily decrease the cost to $4,000,000. I realize the pressure to hire can at times be great. After all, production always trumps HR best practices. When you factor in the increased sales needed to overcome an expedient hire for the sake of production, it is not hard to justify placing a firewall to weed out potential bad hires.

I like to explain the firewall this way. Businesses understand the need to have a firewall for their computers. As organizations become more reliant on computers, the threats to system security have increased. Accordingly, organizations devote increased resources to prevent a virus. It has always boggled my mind that employers do not spend the same time and resources safeguarding their business from what I call a "personal virus," which infects your organization when a bad hire is introduced to the mix. A personal virus can manifest itself in many ways. According to a CareerBuilder survey, when classifying what makes someone a bad hire, employers reported several behavioral and performance-related issues:

- Quality of work was lackluster (67%)
- Failure to work well with other employees (60%)
- Negative attitude (59%)
- Attendance problems (54%)
- Complaints from customers (44%)
- Failure to meet deadlines (44%)[2]

These are all indirect costs. From a risk management standpoint, the direct cost could be a work comp claim or damage to equipment, and the indirect costs could be OSHA fines, loss of productivity because the person is out of work, or impact on productivity of other employees. So what can you do to build a firewall?

A complete workers' compensation employment program involves more than just dealing with claims for workers' compensation injuries. A complete program begins with the hiring process. Compliance with other requirements, such as the Americans with Disabilities Act (ADA), will assist you in dealing with workers' compensation employment issues.

Section 2.1.1
Pre-employment Testing

Integrity Testing

Since one of the primary roles of the prescreening process is to avoid bad hires, integrity testing can be a very cost-effective tool. The integrity test targets negative behaviors—such as abuse of alcohol or drugs, hostility or violence in the workplace, lying or deception in the workplace, and employee theft. All of these "negative factors" have an impact on workers' compensation claims. When you consider that 73 percent of all current illegal drug users aged eighteen and older are employed you need to ask yourself what safeguards do you have in place to protect your organization. The integrity test is such a proven tool that one integrity test vendor claims can reduce work comp costs up to 60 percent.

A 2011 Pacific University study looked at more than 33,000 job applicants from four separate industries (publishing, nursing homes, food processing, and auto club) over a twelve- to thirty-four-month period. The study hypothesized that screened employees would have fewer and less costly claims than unscreened employees. The applicants screened for integrity testing in this study exhibited a 23 percent reduction in claims severity.[3] The Center for Hospitality Research published an article where the authors looked at data from 29,000 would-be employees hired at a hotel chain over a one-year period. The new hires were administered an integrity test. From the pool of 29,000 just under 6,100 were hired. "The screened hires experienced a markedly lower incidence of claims compared to the unscreened, existing employees. The average cost per claim for the unscreened employees was $3,446 as compared to $2,119 for the screened group."[4] When you consider that new hires have a much higher incident rate than existing employees this is significant! The cost of an integrity test is typically in the twelve to twenty dollar range.

Section 2.1.2
The Employment Application Process

The Job Application

Your job application should be a standardized form and must be completed in full by all prospective employees. Here are some best practices.

- ☐ Develop or purchase an application form that solicits important information for your company and is compliant with federal and state regulations. Require all job applicants to complete the application and review the applications before interviewing candidates.

- ☐ Look for gaps or inconsistencies in job history and for date mismatches. An extended period of unemployment or inconsistent dates can indicate lengthy unemployment or incarceration. Date mismatches can indicate that the candidate is not telling the truth.

- ☐ Look for frequent job changes, which could indicate multiple firings or that the employee could be hard to retain.

- ☐ Look for lack of progression or actual regression in job responsibilities and titles. This could indicate lack of potential and initiative, or could signal performance problems.

- ☐ Look for an admission of criminal convictions or other hints that the candidate may have been incarcerated, such as extended gaps in employment (see above).

- ☐ Look for a missing or unintelligible Social Security number, which could indicate the applicant is an illegal alien.

- ☐ Look to see if approval for background check or information on the previous employer is missing. If so, the applicant may be hiding a criminal history, dismissal for cause, or other issues.

- ☐ Look to see if the applicant's driver's license has been revoked, which could indicate substance abuse problems or other legal issues.

- ☐ Look for frequent changes of address, which could indicate instability, an illegal alien, or other troubles with the law.

- ☐ Look for incomplete sections, errors in spelling, sloppiness, and failure to follow instructions in each application. These could indicate sloppiness in work habits, carelessness, or inability to follow instructions. These could also indicate language or reading problems, which may or may not disqualify a candidate.

- ☐ Look at the reasons given for leaving jobs to check for any indication of performance or interpersonal skill issues.[5]

Have a list of interview questions that your HR department will use. These should take into consideration the industry and level of employee you are hiring. This is a good reminder that you should always have your HR attorney review all your policies and procedures *before* you implement them. The interview question list should also include a list of questions you should not ask. I get this question a lot. What questions can and can I not ask? There is no simple answer to this question. Be careful that the questions you ask cannot be misinterpreted as discriminatory. Any information requested from the candidate should be directly related to the position he or she is interviewing for to avoid litigation. Acceptable topics include previous work experience, education, and skills that are necessary for the position being applied for.

COMPOINTS

> IF YOU PURCHASED AN EMPLOYMENT PRACTICE LIABILITY POLICY, YOU MAY HAVE ACCESS TO A FREE HR HOTLINE THAT COULD INCLUDE ACCESS TO LEGAL COUNSEL.

interview. The focus of the interview should be on the job as outlined in the job description (including the physical demands required by the job). In addition to being required to explain how job duties and tasks will be performed, an applicant can also be asked to demonstrate how he or she would perform the particular task. Every employer's goal is to hire the best-qualified applicant, and the proper use of a written job description can assist an employer in achieving that goal.

Developing Job Descriptions

When you develop your job descriptions, you can either hire a company to review your jobs and write your job descriptions or you can develop them in-house. If you develop them in-house, we strongly recommend that you have your employment attorney review the job descriptions and how you use those job descriptions within your organization. If you choose to develop a job description in-house, a good resource tool is www.jobdescriptions.com. This is an online software tool that contains over 5,000 job descriptions, and is an easy and effective way to build job descriptions. You can either purchase the software or use their online service, or you can hire a third party vendor that specializes in developing job descriptions. BLR also has a job description builder but it does not include physical demands, so I don't use it unless I have a third party come in and develop the physical demands analysis (PDA).

The two most critical parts of the job description are the **essential functions** and the **physical demands analysis.**

Essential Functions

Defining the Essential Functions:

Employers who are subject to the ADA should verify each **essential function definition** meet the ADA definition of an essential duty. Even employers who are not subject to the ADA will find these guidelines helpful in deciding exactly which essential functions to include.

For more information about the ADA, see Americans with Disabilities Act, Title I.[7] The ADA considers a job function essential if:

- The position exists to perform that function.
- There are only a limited number of employees available among whom the performance of that function can be distributed.
- The function is so highly specialized that the person in the position is hired for his or her expertise or ability to perform the particular function.

Under the ADA, you can use the following considerations as you establish the **essential functions** and qualifications for a job:

Process

- ☐ The work experience of past incumbents
- ☐ The current work experience of incumbents in similar jobs
- ☐ The amount of time spent on the job performing the function
- ☐ The effect of removing the function from the job
- ☐ The terms of a collective bargaining agreement

The 80/20 Rule:

Probably the most difficult aspect of preparing job descriptions is deciding what functions, duties, and responsibilities to include. It may be hard for someone not intimately familiar with the job to determine which job activities are truly "essential" and which are marginal or incidental. One rule some employers have followed states that 80 percent of what comes out of a job is the result of 20 percent of what goes into it. In other words, only about 20 percent of what the employee actually does is responsible for achieving 80 percent of the job's results or objectives. The significant point to remember here is that it is this 20 percent of the job's content that you are trying to capture in the essential functions of the job description.

There is no substitute for experience when it comes to writing job descriptions. All the advice, rules, guidelines, and suggested formats presented thus far will be meaningless until they are applied. And because jobs themselves vary so widely, it is impossible to provide a step-by-step guide to writing the "ideal" job description. The best approach is to reread and assimilate what has been said up to this point and then tackle the first job, preferably a low-level one that is limited in scope and lends itself to a fairly concrete description. Some employers ask an employee currently performing the essential functions of the job to help them gather information to develop the job description.

Detailing Essential Functions Descriptions:

When defining the essential duties of a job, try focusing on the result to be accomplished, rather than on a precise method (unless the method is an inseparable part of the job). In this way, you are better prepared to evaluate whether a reasonable accommodation can be made to enable an otherwise qualified individual with a disability to perform the job.

EXAMPLE

An essential function of a mailroom clerk job is to move packages on and off shelves. Some of the shelves are six feet high.

> *POOR:* Places and retrieves packages by standing on feet and reaching up to six-foot-high shelves.

> *BETTER:* Places and retrieves packages on shelves.

By stating the result (what needs to be accomplished) and not focusing on the method (how it will get done), you are writing an essential function statement free of possible discriminatory language.

However, under the Physical Demands section, you would want to include the need to reach and lift from six-foot shelves as well as the weight of the packages. Then, if you were dealing with an otherwise qualified individual with a disability that prevented him or her from reaching that high, you would need to consider whether there is a reasonable accommodation that would enable the person to perform this essential function. Possible accommodations might include lowering the shelf height or providing a step stool.

Tips for Writing Essential Functions:

- ☐ Get thorough input from multiple sources about the job duties. Consider using a questionnaire form as your data collection method.

- ☐ Include duties performed frequently and occupy the greatest proportion of the work. Provide the most detail about these duties.

- ☐ Include duties performed infrequently, but must be done on a scheduled basis (such as weekly, monthly, or even annually) and are important to accomplishing the job's primary purpose.

  > *POOR:* Writes monthly report of accomplishments.

  > *BETTER:* Compiles semi-monthly payroll data. Supervises production of company's annual report.

- ☐ Include duties performed irregularly, but are important to accomplishing the job's primary purpose.

  > *POOR:* Clears printer jams if jams occur while printing documents.

  > *BETTER:* Implements disaster recovery program for company computer systems in the event of an emergency.

Process

- Start the statement with an action verb that describes the worker's action in specific terms rather than using vague or ambiguous words. Use the present tense, rather than past or passive.

    POOR: Handles mail. Provides financial information. After completing telephone calls, entered information into the database.

    BETTER: Sorts and distributes mail. Prepares budgets and financial reports. Updates database with information from telephone calls.

- Describe what the worker does, not what the tools or methods do.

    POOR: Carries freight. Stamps out metal parts of toys with punch press. Computerizes inventory.

    BETTER: Drives truck that carries freight. Feeds metal into punch press that stamps out parts of toys. Writes computer programs that store inventory information.

- Use job titles and organizational units rather than specific names when describing job interrelationships.

    POOR: Gives order forms to Mary for data entry. Audits accounts of Des Moines and Cedar Falls offices.

    BETTER: Gives order forms to Order Department for data entry. Audits branch offices' accounts.

- Use simple, concise terms and phrases that are clear to employees, management, human resources, and anyone else who may use the job description. Because job descriptions may be seen by people such as applicants who do not know the job, use language that will also be clear to outsiders whenever possible.

    POOR: Completes SI forms 456 and 456A.

    BETTER: Completes sales information forms for initial orders and order cancellations.

- Combine tasks into one duty statement when they are related and produce the same result. (However, beware of combining too many steps into one duty.)

    POOR: Mixes dough. Kneads dough. Forms dough into loaves. Places loaves in oven.

    BETTER: Mixes and kneads dough, forming into loaves, and placing in oven to bake.

Physical Demands Analysis

The physical demands analysis (PDA) is an important pre-hire tool, and is a critical part of a successful return to work (RTW) process. We will talk about the RTW process in great detail later in the program, but consider, if RTW is predicated on the job description (including the PDA) and the employer doesn't have a written job description, who then is left to make up the job description? You guessed it—the injured employee. Talk about a huge cost driver! If you do not have well-written job descriptions including PDAs, your lost time days will be higher than they should be!

Legal Impact of Physical Demands Analysis:

The Physical Demands section describes the physical skills and abilities an employee typically must have to perform the job successfully. In completing this section, you will want to be sure that you can relate all physical demands to the essential job duties.

Physical demand standards can have legal significance if they are the basis for selection decisions challenged under the ADA or other employment laws. Being clear about a job's physical demands during the interview process will help to surface any restrictions or accommodation needs. If a physical demand screens out individuals protected by employment legislation, the employer must be prepared to show that the standard is "job related and consistent with business necessity." The employer must consider making a reasonable accommodation to enable an otherwise qualified individual with a disability to perform the job. Therefore, when describing physical demands, it is important to link them closely to the job's essential duties. Ask yourself what requirements an employee must meet for strength, agility, mobility, and sensory abilities in order to perform the job effectively and safely.

Creating Physical Demands Analysis:

IF YOU HAVE YOUR PHYSICAL DEMANDS BROKEN DOWN INTO TASKS WITH VIDEO YOU WILL GET EMPLOYEES BACK TO WORK QUICKER.

You can certainly do this yourself. But be careful. The accuracy of the PDA will be scrutinized if you use it as part of your employment or RTW process. I use a third party to develop my clients' job descriptions. We have developed a format that breaks out each task, which makes the physical demands very granular. We also embed short video clips or pictures that depict the task. Why is this important? It certainly gives the prospective new hire a better understanding of the physical demands of the job they are applying for, which if coupled with the post-offer health questionnaire, could prevent the placement of an employee into a position that will most likely result in a claim. For return to work, the granularity of breaking down the physical demands into tasks will give the Authorized Treating Physician more options to return the employee

Process

back to work. Rather than saying an injured employee cannot return to full duty, they can pick certain tasks the employee can or cannot do. Regardless of how you build job descriptions, having the PDA completed before the injury will significantly reduce days away from work.

Section 2.1.4

Drug-free Workplace

Being a drug-free workplace is so important it is referenced in P1 through P4. According to the National Institute on Drug Abuse, nearly 75 percent of all adult illicit drug users are employed. Studies show that when compared with non-substance abusers, substance-abusing employees are more likely to:

- Change jobs frequently
- Be late to or absent from work
- Be less productive employees
- Be involved in a workplace accident
- File a workers' compensation claim[8]

Studies show that drugs in the workplace cost employers billions. Simply put, if you do not have an effective drug-free workplace program you will become the employer of choice for drug users. So why do I have this listed under P1. If you haven't done this already, you should post a big sign where it is very visible to new hires that you are a drug-free workplace. You may never really have any tangible proof, but you will have applicants see the sign and turn around and leave. You have to establish a firewall to keep out undesirable potential employees that can negatively impact your safety culture, and this posting will help.

In most instances, a drug-free workplace may mean you only test on a post-accident basis. Many states have a certified drug-free workplace designation you can apply for that may qualify for a discount (typically a 5–7.5 percent premium credit). The basic components of most states certifications are:

- A written policy
- Access to assistance
- Employee education

- ☐ Supervisor training
- ☐ Drug testing

If you are not a certified drug-free workplace, you should discuss all the benefits with your broker. For example, in many states having a certified drug-free workplace may strengthen your ability to deny or controvert a claim.

COMPOINTS

> PREDATORS SEEK OUT EMPLOYERS WHO DON'T SCREEN THEIR NEW HIRES. AN EFFECTIVE FIREWALL FOR STOPPING THESE PREDATORS STARTS AT P1.

Section 2.2

P2 Post-offer

Workers' Compensation information is considered health and disability related under the American's with Disabilities Act (ADA). We have a chapter dedicated to the interplay between ADA/FMLA/WC. In order to comply with this federal act, an employer must NOT ask any questions about an applicant for employment that is connected with health and disability unless, and until, the employer has made a conditional job offer to the employee applicant or has made an actual job offer that is NOT tentative.

Once a job offer has been made, an employer may pursue information about health or disability if such inquiry is related to the specific job and performance requirements. This information should be asked for on a separate health and disability questionnaire, completed by the applicant only AFTER the conditional or permanent job offer has been made.

Previous Workers' Compensation filings are NOT grounds to refuse employment to an applicant, but the safety implications are apparent and should be considered. Please keep in mind any advice given in this book should be reviewed by your legal counsel before implementation.

Process

Your P2 process needs to work in coordination with P1. Hopefully, you have gathered a lot of information in P1 and made an informed decision to make a conditional offer. Now you have to go through your post-offer considerations. In this section, we will discuss post-offer testing and health questionnaire and new hire safety orientation.

Section 2.2.1

Post-offer Testing

Drug Testing

Most drug-free certification programs require post-offer drug testing. A failed drug test may allow you to withdraw the job offer. Please note that each state may have specific guidelines on the types of testing that are permissible. Also, drug test results should be considered confidential and maintained in a separate file from employee personnel files. Here are three testing options:

1. Instant tests are the most affordable option. If a positive test result occurs, the employee should have the right to pay for another test at a laboratory of their choice (SAMSHA Certified).
2. You could sign up with a third party service to do your confirmatory test in-house and ship the test results off to a certified lab.
3. You could send the applicant to a SAMSHA certified lab.

Compliance Testing

Instant Searches:

Many employers will do an immediate "instant search." This will pull up data like SSN and address history, a criminal index, and if the person shows up in the multi-state sex offender index. This instant search is a key to helping you determine what additional tests you should order. For example, if the application lists that the employee has lived in Georgia the past seven years but the address verification shows that the employee has actually lived in two other states in addition to Georgia, they may be hiding something. Additionally, if you were doing verification on whether the employee has filed previous workers' compensation claims, if you relied on the employment application you might only check Georgia, but with the address history, you will have a flag to check the other states.

Criminal:

Best practices to conduct criminal background checks can vary widely depending on the employer. I do a lot of work in the poultry industry. Most are not too concerned about petty crimes, but I certainly do not want to see my client hire a person with a violent criminal history in a plant where the employees are wielding knives. I have another client who manufactures and installs custom shutters. Since their employees are in customers' homes, the need for a background check is pretty apparent. But this is not just for blue-collar jobs. I have had a number of my clients victimized by employee theft. This ranges from theft of product to embezzlement.

The Association of Certified Fraud Examiners (ACFE) reported in 2012 that small businesses suffered a "disproportionately large" median loss of $147,000 from embezzlement claims.[9] On average, it takes eighteen months for an employer to catch an employee who is stealing.[10] In "How to Prevent Small Business Fraud: A Manual for Business Professionals," CFE cites two key factors that contribute to the large losses suffered by small companies—lack of basic accounting controls and a greater degree of misplaced trust. More often than not, it is the long-trusted employee—typically, the small business's one-person accounting department—who is found to be the thief. In other words, the person you least suspect is usually the one who commits the crime.[11]

Most insurance contracts that cover employee dishonesty require the employer to press charges to submit a claim. But our court system is inundated, and most guilty convictions result in a hand slap. All of this makes background checks even more important. If you go in and tell your staff that you are conducting criminal background checks and someone balks, you may have some issues. Also, just as a side note, but with the increased exposure to employee theft this might be a good time to review your insurance coverage for employee dishonesty coverage.

Verifications:

This could vary depending on the position and company. Verification searches could include: past employment, education, reference checks, social validation, and workers' compensation. I want to focus on a couple of these.

- ☐ Past employment – This will give you a pretty good idea of the person's integrity if you match this up with their employment application. The cost of a new hire is expensive and if the employee hops jobs every few months are they really someone you want to hire? Also, if they lie about the employment history it should be a very large red flag.
- ☐ Workers' Compensation – Since workers' compensation is administered on a state-by-state basis you will have to run these reports on a state-by-state basis. We previously discussed the importance of the address verification earlier to prompt you to run reports on each applicable state. Most states reports will give you the time of incident, type of injury, body

part, and job-related disability. Depending on the state reporting, however, information may vary. Below are some common uses for workers' comp reports.

- Determine if an applicant has falsified their medical history
- Coupled with the post-offer health questionnaire, make an educated decision if an applicant cannot perform essential job functions with reasonable accommodations
- Prevent someone with a high frequency of claims from posing a safety danger to other employees
- Background investigations of accident victim for previous injuries/claims (typically, this is done by the Insurer/TPA on a post-accident basis)
- Discover the location of employers left off the job application due to Workers' Compensation claims

Section 2.2.2

Post-offer Health Questionnaire

COMPOINTS

> IT IS INTERESTING THAT LABOR ATTORNEYS USUALLY SAY DON'T USE A POST-OFFER HEALTH QUESTIONNAIRE AND DEFENSE ATTORNEYS ALMOST ALWAYS RECOMMEND USING ONE!

Wade McGuffey with Goodman, McGuffey, Lindsey, and Johnson assisted with the section on the post-offer health questionnaire. We discussed job descriptions earlier in the chapter. The recommended best practice is to have a written job description (including the PDA) at the pre-employment stage of hiring. If the job is offered, the appropriate screening should take place and the employee should be given a post-offer health questionnaire.

I understand that there is a huge explosion of litigation related to employment practices. But I strongly recommend using the post-offer health questionnaire. I have been using the same post-offer health questionnaire for about eighteen years and it is actively in use by thousands of employers. I do not have any knowledge that the form has ever resulted in an EEOC action. Your broker will more than likely have a form that they can provide for you. Please remember you should consult your legal counsel *before* you implement or utilize any form, policy, or procedure.

Below is some guidance from Wade on how to properly use the form.

Utilizing a Health History Questionnaire

(You need to check state-specific guidelines to see if you can utilize the form in states other than Georgia.)

The use of health history questionnaires and medical examinations in the workplace may be appropriate; however, an employer needs to be careful when asking prospective employees and current employees about their medical history. Medical information regarding a prospective employee or current employee's medical history must be obtained in compliance with the standards outlined by the EEOC and the Americans with Disabilities Act.

The EEOC does not provide general guidance on all workers' compensation matters. The workers' compensation laws in each state are different and may have different applications and interactions with federal law. The ADA is federal law and would govern in the case of a conflict. In many states, there is not a conflict between the Workers' Compensation Act and the ADA. It is clear that an employer can make a job offer to a prospective employee contingent upon completion of a health history questionnaire, and the employer's motives for doing so cannot be questioned so long as the employer requires every new employee in the same job category to complete the health history questionnaire.

Directing current employees to complete a medical health history questionnaire is more problematic. The EEOC does not give any specific guidance on requiring current employees to complete a medical health history questionnaire. Requiring current employees to complete a health history questionnaire should be done only when the inquiry is job-related and necessary for the business. Of course, any health or medical information obtained from an employee or prospective employee must be maintained on separate forms, in a separate medical file, and must be treated as a confidential medical record. With the above in mind, below are some guidelines for using health history questionnaires and medical examinations for each type of employee.

New Employees

The law is clear and undisputed that a health history questionnaire can be required of all new employees once a job offer has been made. "A covered entity may require medical examination (and/or inquiry) after making an offer of employment to a job applicant and before the applicant begins his/her employment duties, and may condition an offer of employment on the results of such examination (and/or inquiry), if all entering employees of the same job category are subjected to such an examination (and/or inquiry) regardless of disability."[12] "Medical examinations conducted in accordance with this section do not have to be job-related and consistent with business necessity."[13]

Under federal law, therefore, while a medical history questionnaire may not be required to be completed pre-employment, any offer of employment may be conditioned upon the completion of such a questionnaire. The EEOC has made it clear that the ADA does not require an employer to justify its requirement that each new employee complete a health history questionnaire. The ADA does require, however, that any information obtained from the post-offer health history questionnaire be used only in compliance with the ADA. An employer may not refuse to hire or revoke the offer of employment based upon information obtained from a post-offer medical examination or inquiry unless the reason for not hiring the individual is job related and necessary for the business. In order to show that the reason for not hiring the individual is job related and necessary for the business, the employer must show that no reasonable accommodation was available to enable the individual to perform the essential functions of the job or that any accommodation would impose an undue hardship on the employer.[14]

The ADA also requires that any information regarding a medical condition or history that is collected be maintained on separate forms, in a separate medical file, and be treated as a confidential medical record.[15] Someone with hiring authority, of course, must review the medical information, but solely for the purpose of determining whether further inquiries should be made, and to determine whether reasonable accommodation should be considered.

For example in Georgia, because it is undisputed that a health history questionnaire can be required of any new employee post-offer, every job offer in Georgia should be contingent upon the completion of a health history questionnaire.

Current Employees

After a person starts work, a medical examination or inquiry must be job-related and necessary for the business.[16] It is clear that disability-related questions, medical examinations, or health history questionnaires are appropriate when an employee seeks to return to work following an injury.[17]

The ADA allows medical monitoring to meet standards established by federal, state, or local laws.[18] The ADA does not overrule state or local laws, except when there is a conflict. "This provision also permits periodic physicals to determine fitness for duty or other medical monitoring if such physicals or monitoring is required by medical standards or requirements established by federal, state, or local laws that are consistent with the ADA."[19]

If an employer has questions about a current employee's ability to return to work following a work injury, a fit for duty exam can be scheduled, but must comply with the ADA. Using it solely to obtain knowledge about the employee's ability to return to work at a suitable job in compliance with the Workers' Compensation Act certainly can be both job-related and serves a legitimate business purpose. As with new employees, any health or medical information from a current employee must also be maintained on separate forms, in a separate medical file, and must be treated as confidential medical records.

Testing Applicants

The ADA does not restrict an employer's right to establish job qualifications. An employer may establish physical or mental qualifications necessary to perform the job. Standards that are intended to exclude an entire class of individuals with disabilities, however, are prohibited. Standards that measure a physical or mental ability needed to perform a job are allowed. A physical agility test to determine physical qualifications necessary for certain jobs prior to making a job offer are allowable if they are in fact simply an agility test and not a medical examination. An agility test, however, may not involve a medical examination or diagnosis by a physician and may not require the revealing of any medical or health history other than to ask whether the person can safely perform the test.[20]

An employer may not, however, use qualification standards, employment tests, or other selection criteria that screen out or tend to screen out an individual with a disability or a class of individuals with disability. Any such standard, test, or criteria must be shown to be job related and consistent with business necessity.[21]

Risk Management Considerations

It is important to have the form in English and Spanish. Also, if the employee cannot read, someone needs to verbally explain the form, sign that they attest that the form was explained, and the employee understood the purpose of the form. We will talk about claims action plans later in the book. The post-offer health questionnaire should be reviewed on every claim. If the employee falsified the questionnaire and that becomes relevant to the work comp claim, your insurance carrier or TPA may be able to deny benefits. Please remember to send a copy to your adjuster. Adjusters typically have a narrow time frame (many states is twenty-one days) to accept or deny a claim. So getting them a copy of the questionnaire timely is crucial. We will talk more about this in P4 Post claims management. As with any health information, the post-offer health questionnaire needs to be kept in a separate file from the employee application.

Section 2.2.3
Safety Quotient

There are numerous published studies that show unsafe physical hazards account for 10 percent of all the workplace injuries. The other 90 percent are caused by unsafe behavior. But addressing behavior can be an incredibly complex task. One tool we have found to assist is the Safety Quotient. They offer an assessment tool where the applicant completes a ten to fifteen minute assessment. Whereas the Integrity Test is designed to test applicants (recommended on a pre-hire basis) to avoid making a bad hire, the Safety Quotient assessment can be a very useful tool to help you with your organization's

Process

Safety IQ. The purpose of this report is to provide information on this person's potential safety risks and offers suggestions to help the employee stay safe in the workplace.

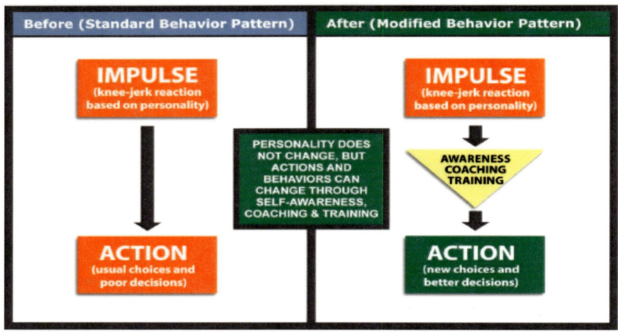

© 2013 TalentClick Workforce Solutions Inc.

The Safety Quotient assessment renders a report for the employer and the employee to use for coaching and development. Most employers use the Safety Quotient assessment on a post-offer basis for coaching and training opportunities and typically do not use as a tool to withdraw the job offer, unless the job is in a safety sensitive area.

Below is a sample profile from the TalentClick Safety Quotient.

Overall Result: This person's S.Q. score is 55 which is in the Average Risk category.

	Overall Risk Level		
	Lower Risk (75-100)	Average Risk (25-74)	Higher Risk (0-24)
S.Q. (Safety Quotient)™: An overall score based on the results on the five safety scales below. S.Q. Scores range from 1-100. SQ scores closer to 100 indicate this person is more likely to engage in safe behaviors. **55**		✓	

Detailed Results:

Safety Risk Factors	Risk Level		
	Lower Risk	Average Risk	Higher Risk
Resistant: Higher risk individuals may disregard authority and rules and be resistant to feedback. Lower risk individuals tend to willingly follow guidelines, follow training and are compliant with rules.	▉		
Anxious: Higher risk individuals may panic or freeze when faced with unexpected safety-sensitive situations, and may feel unsure about their abilities. Lower risk individuals tend to be confident and are steady and calm under pressure.		▉▉▉▉▉▉▉▉▉	
Irritable: Higher risk individuals may become annoyed by others especially when under stress. Lower risk individuals tend to be less irritable and are easily able to control their emotions when under stress.		▉▉▉▉▉▉▉▉▉▉	
Distractible: Higher risk individuals seek stimulation and variety, and may be easily distracted. Lower risk individuals are less likely to seek stimulation and are able to stay focused and alert.	▉▉		
Impulsive: Higher risk individuals tend to seek excitement, enjoy taking risks and may underestimate possible negative consequences of their actions. Lower risk individuals do not seek excitement and tend to carefully evaluate their options before making decisions.	▉		
	Lower Risk	Average Risk	Higher Risk

We cannot predict the occurrence of specific incidents. We can only predict the possibility that people will engage in certain behaviors which, if they persist, will make incidents likely. These assessment results should always be considered in the context of all available information about a person and should not be used as the sole factor for making employment-related decisions.

© 2013 TalentClick Workforce Solutions Inc.

So how does the Safety Quotient test help? Although you can change behavior over time, people are driven by impulses based on their own unique personality. People's impulses (or personality) typically don't change. The test results help the employer and the employee better understand how these personality traits can positively or negatively impact your safety culture. When the employee completes the assessment, it generates an employer report with sample questions to help coach the employee and address safety culture issues. The employee also gets a self-help sheet to help them address their own safety concerns. I believe this interaction with the employee during the new hire process is a great way to evidence your commitment to your organization's safety culture. The results can also facilitate our two-step new hire safety orientation process by making the employer aware of safety risk factors so they can address them in the orientation process. If your organization has safety sensitive jobs, this could be an effective resource to improve your Safety IQ.

Section 2.2.4

New Hire Safety Orientation

Statistics generally state that about 40 percent of all workplace injuries happen during the first year of employment.[22] My experience shows that industries with high turnover may have stats that are as high as 80 percent. Wow. That is a big number. Why do new hires have such a high accident rate? Well, the easy answer is most employers do not have adequate training. Here are the top excuses for not having an effective new hire safety orientation:

- ☐ **I simply do not have the resources to conduct the training.**

    This is understandable. Employers are having to do more with less so everybody is stretched thin.

- ☐ **We stick them in front of a DVD for three hours and show them all the required training, isn't that enough?**

    You have lost the employee after maybe ten minutes. Sure, you have a record for OSHA, but how much did the employee learn?

- ☐ **I can't keep up with all the regulatory changes.**

    I must admit the Federal Government (OSHA) doesn't always make it easy for employers. But most brokers have access to good reference resources to help you. I will give you detailed resources later in the book.

- ☐ **I rely on my insurance carrier.**

    This won't work. While your insurance carrier can provide you important resources to help, in most cases they cannot provide adequate training—mostly because of logistics.

They may only make two visits a year. What happens in the interim? Also, they are not usually connected to the safety culture (how could they be with limited interactions). The insurance carriers can and should be involved in ongoing training within your organization. They just may not be the best resource to conduct your new hire training.

Incident rates are high with new hires so you must evidence your organization's commitment to safety in the new hire process. Here are some reasons why that is so important:

- Employers assume new employees know more than they really do—and that common sense will prevent most accidents. (You know what they say about the word assume?)
- New employees are afraid to ask questions.
- Younger employees may feel they are invincible.
- Older employees may feel they know it already.
- Lack of commitment. Commitment is a two-way street. If an organization has not invested in its safety culture, how can you expect the employee to?

Regardless of the reason, if you want to take one step to lower your workers' comp costs you should focus on your new hire safety orientation. Many organizations that reinvent their new hire safety orientation have their entire organization go through the training. I use a two-step process to conduct the new hire training. The first part is a safety video (I like it to be as short as possible, customized, and branded to the client's specific needs). Part two is a supervisor-led safety walkthrough. We will cover this in much greater detail in the chapter devoted to training.

Section 2.3

P3 Prevention

> PREVENTION REQUIRES VIGILANCE. VIGILANCE REQUIRES MANAGEMENT COMMITMENT.

Process

Imagine if you could invest one dollar in your business process and get a return of four to six dollars. OSHA states that every dollar invested in safety yields a four to six dollar return.

We have talked a lot about workers' compensation and claims, but have talked little about prevention. When it comes to workers' compensation, prevention is usually associated with loss control, which is typically called risk prevention.

As we go through this chapter, I want you to focus on the definitions of risk and prevention.

> **RISK –** Chance of something going wrong: the danger that injury, damage, or loss will occur.
>
> **PREVENTION –** Something that acts to prevent something: an action that makes it impossible or very difficult for somebody to do something or for something to happen.

Consider risk as when something goes wrong and prevention as taking an action to prevent injury. Most safety efforts focus on physical hazards, but as we previously mentioned, only 10 percent of workplace injuries are caused by unsafe physical hazards. The other 90 percent are due to behavior.

So to prevent risk, shouldn't most of the effort focus on behavior? Behavior based safety (BBS) is not a new concept, but most organizations fail to implement a BBS program. This book is not meant to be a treatise on BBS. There are dozens of really good books on this topic. But BBS is an undercurrent that you will feel throughout this book. We have already talked about BBS in P2—when we outlined the Safety Quotient. BBS is also a huge cost driver in P3. Certainly physical hazards in certain industries pose more risk. But regardless of the industry, *behavior* will always be the biggest cost driver! If you want to prevent claims, you have to impact behavior. When safety is the main thing, it permeates the entire organization; therefore, whether it is a production meeting, an HR meeting, or any employee gathering, safety needs to be the first item on the agenda. Also, safety does not stop and start at work. Organizations that stress prevention away from work have a much better chance of making the message resonate while the employee is at work.

Here is another interesting twist on prevention. A huge cost driver in workers' compensation comes from litigated claims. Most claimant attorneys know the pressure points to try to force a settlement. If an injured employee retains counsel, you have probably lost the battle. But here is an important reminder. You have an opportunity to gain the employee's trust before the accident happens. This does not sound like a typical prevention strategy, but we will discuss it at length in the chapter on organization.

COMPOINTS

> ORGANIZATIONS WITH POSITIVE SAFETY CULTURES HAVE LESS EMPLOYEE LITIGATION. THIS EXTENDS BEYOND WORKERS' COMP TO EMPLOYMENT PRACTICES CLAIMS!

Section 2.3.1
Safety Training

In this section, we will discuss safety training, safety assessments, employee perception surveys, performance reviews, and supervisor training.

Have you ever read Stephen Covey's book *The 7 Habits of Highly Effective People*? The book clearly explains the direct correlation between safety, productivity, fewer incidents, and better quality. Many people are risk takers. Managing risk relies on prevention, and prevention is a learned skill. I think training is so critical that I have devoted a whole chapter in the book to this topic.

Section 2.3.2
Safety Committees

Safety committees are nothing new. In fact, when I entered the insurance industry thirty-two years ago, safety committees were more prevalent than they are today. Communication has a strong influence over your organization's safety culture and the safety committee serves as a two-way channel of communication, and to promote safety awareness throughout the workplace.

Organization

The Safety & Health Committee will consist of supervisors representing each division or department along with representation from the employees and management. The Safety & Health Committee will meet

Process

monthly/quarterly/semiannually/annually. The meeting will be chaired by the safety coordinator. Should a scheduled meeting have to be postponed, it will be held later in the month, on a date and time determined by the safety coordinator.

Function

The Safety & Health Committee has the following functions:

- Review the safety audits.
- Review and update safety rules and safe operating procedures.
- Review accidents and "near miss" incidents reported since the last meeting, and suggest means for preventing future occurrences.
- Convey, review, and comment on safety suggestions submitted by employees.
- Plan and carry out various safety promotion activities (such as contests, award programs, perception surveys, etc.).
- Promote safety awareness among all employees through safe attitudes and day-to-day interactions. The safety committee has to lead by example.

Here are some tips for forming a safety committee:

- Take into account an employee's personal experience with safety when selecting Safety & Health Committee members. Someone from a specific work area with a history of accident or injury problems can bring valuable insights to the committee.
- Volunteers or individuals who show they have an interest in safety are also good candidates. Likewise, individuals with a good safety record can bring their own experience to the group.
- Rotate membership so that members exposed to Safety & Health Committee issues are "circulated" back into the workforce and others are brought in.
- Occasionally, specialists or consultants may be added to the committee to address a specific situation or problem. This will breathe life into the safety committee. The insurance carrier's risk control department can be a great (free) resource.
- Written documentation of Safety & Health Committee meetings should be maintained. A log or written minutes should be taken at each meeting. Meetings should follow a standard

agenda. This is the number one reason safety committees fail, because there is not a set agenda. Having a set agenda gives the committee an expectation of what will be covered. This consistency will create accountability. Accountability will improve your organization's safety culture.

Here is a sample safety committee planner that I developed.

Safety Meeting Agenda Planner   Date_____

Welcome Remarks _____

_____

_____

_____

Trend Review (month and year to date)

    Lag time report

    Cause of Injury

    Body part

    Locations/Departments

    Root cause Analysis

    Med only/Lost time

Accident Review

    Claim: Employee_____ Accident Date_____

    Action Plan: _____

_____

    Claim: Employee_____ Accident Date_____

    Action Plan: _____

_____

    Claim: Employee_____ Accident Date_____

    Action Plan: _____

_____

Process

Safety Topic for meeting (attach copy of documents): _____
_____
_____

Action Plan for next meeting: _____
_____
_____

Section 2.3.3

Safety Assessments

If you have a safety audit process in place, the first thing I would do is replace the word *audit* with the word *assessment*. The word audit can have a negative connotation. If you are currently conducting an assessment, how is it perceived? I recently did a walkthrough with a new client. They have two young safety officers that are really doing a great job. One of the things they do as they go through their weekly safety audit is snap pictures. They use these pictures in their monthly safety meetings. What a great idea! It has created much higher safety awareness. Since this process has been going on for a year or so, I asked them how they are received when they walkthrough the different plants. They stated employees and supervisors definitely know who they are! I asked if that was a good thing, and they responded with a shrug! I continued my questions, and asked if most of the assessment items reviewed were in compliance or out of compliance. They commented that the compliance rate has markedly improved since they started the process. They said their compliance rate is now above 95 percent, which is awesome. I then posed a simple question. How often do they pull employees or supervisors aside and commend them for doing a good job when they observe safe work practices? Whoa! You mean compliment them for the 95 percent they are doing right, rather than ding them for the 5 percent they are doing wrong! You need to have consequences for unsafe behavior, but you also need to make sure you recognize positive safety behavior.

HAVE THE PERSON COMPLETING THE SAFETY ASSESSMENT COMPLIMENT AN EMPLOYEE OR A SUPERVISOR FOR DOING SOMETHING RIGHT!

I believe in safety assessments and think they are a critical part of an effective workplace safety program, but I do want to throw this out there for consideration. Safety conditions are easy to control. They are pretty straightforward. Behavior, on the other hand, is much more difficult to control. So even with the safety assessment process described below, you need to remember that employees respond better to positive reinforcement than negative reinforcement. You need to have rules, and if an employee refuses to follow them, they should be disciplined, but behavior typically does not change because of discipline. It changes because of buying in! There are six steps to the safety assessment process.

Creating the Safety Assessment

Your insurance carrier is a good start. Chances are the carrier has some good templates they can use to help you build an assessment. When the carrier calls to schedule a risk control meeting tell them that you want assistance building an assessment that fits your organization's specific needs. I also utilize third party resources like Zywave, BLR, and JJ Keller. They all offer some great off-the-shelf templates for most industries.

Conducting a Safety Assessment

There is no right answer. I have some clients that do daily by shift, and some that do weekly. I think the assessment should be done at least every week. But if you create a schedule, keep it. If you start slacking off, the people in your organization will not attach the same value to the assessment.

Analyzing a Safety Assessment

The problem with most safety assessments (even the good ones) is they are paper. Which means as you gather more audits your stack of paper gets larger! As the stack gets larger, the historical data (trending) gets lost in the shuffle. Here are a few tips:

- ☐ Consider doing away with the paper and consider an e-assessment. That is an assessment that can be completed on a tablet or a smartphone.

- ☐ Create a database to measure and manage exceptions. I would recommend managing exceptions three ways. The first exception is whether the audit was completed. The next exception is whether something was out of compliance, and the third exception is whether compliance issue was corrected.

- ☐ If you create a database, you will be able to run reports.

- ☐ If you can run reports, the safety assessment can become part of your safety committee and management meetings.

Action Plan to Correct Deficiencies

If OSHA comes into your organization, they will look for compliance issues. If you consciously know about a hazard in the workplace and don't take corrective action, you can expect a bigger fine from OSHA. Consider that in 2010 OSHA significantly increased the penalties for repeat offenders. Additionally, employers with a history of repeat offenses can expect more frequent OSHA inspections and mandatory follow-up inspections. Beyond the increased vigilance by OSHA, if you are not proactive on your follow-up on deficiencies, employees will quickly discern that safety is not a priority.

Monitoring the Results

IF IT IS NOT BEING MEASURED, IT IS NOT BEING MANAGED!

I can usually identify the person in charge of the safety assessments by the large stack of paper on the floor in the corner of their office. I joke about this, but it is true. After a while, the safety assessment loses its "zing" and the "exceptions" find their place in the corner of the room. In the process I developed, we measure exceptions two ways. The first measurement of an exception is to determine if the assessments are being completed timely. The second is to measure exceptions on the compliance of the actual questions on the assessment. What makes our process a little unique is we roll up the stats from the two exception reports to the management dashboard.

Raise Your Safety IQ

MANAGEMENT MAY NEVER READ THE SAFETY ASSESSMENTS, BUT BY HAVING A WAY TO MEASURE EXCEPTIONS, YOU WILL INCREASE ACCOUNTABILITY.

This is actually easy if you have the right system in place. Here are some tips:

- Make the exception stats part of your regular safety meetings. You may also want the safety committee to periodically conduct an assessment.

- Have someone from senior management periodically conduct a safety assessment. That will accomplish two things. It will show the employees that management cares about safety, and it will tangibly connect management to the safety assessment process.

- Another good tip is to have your risk control specialist from your insurance carrier participate in this process. This will connect them to your safety culture, which will help them better serve you. An added bonus of this tip is that their reports go to underwriting. By involving them in your Safety IQ, the report they submit to underwriting will be more favorable, which could lead to more favorable pricing on your next renewal.

- Benchmark one location against another. It will help you target your training efforts.

Section 2.3.4

Safety Motivation Programs

The topic of safety incentive programs elicit some mixed responses, so I changed the name to safety motivation programs. Twenty years ago, safety incentive programs were all the rage. It made sense and I must admit I was on the bandwagon. My agency had a third party company that handled all of the administration so it was easy for our clients to implement. They sent catalogs home to the spouse to garner interest. This was a powerful communication. The spouses starting getting invested in the company's safety culture. Why? Because they saw something they wanted in the catalog. Participants all went into the pool and the day came for a selection. If an employee was selected and their department had a lost time claim, the employee was automatically relegated to a second or third place prize. It did create some great buzz around safety and did have some success. But in most cases, the "bounce" from the program faded. Sometimes rather quickly! The key to a successful program is to invest in motivation not in incentives. In some extreme cases, because of the peer pressure, accidents were not reported.

This subject was the topic of an OSHA memorandum issued on March 12, 2012, by Richard Fairfax, Deputy Assistant Secretary. In the memo, he cited the whistleblower statute, which states that the practice of retaliating against a worker for reporting an injury or illness is illegal discrimination under section 11(c). Fairfax stated, "If employees do not feel free to report injuries or illnesses, the employer's entire workforce is put at risk. Employers do not learn of and correct dangerous conditions that have resulted in injuries, and injured employees may not receive the proper medical attention, or the workers' compensation benefits to which they are entitled. Ensuring that employees can report injuries or illnesses without fear of retaliation is therefore crucial to protecting worker safety and health."[23]

He goes on to outline four types of workplace practices which could discourage timely reporting of claims, and safety incentive programs was one of the four points. Mr. Fairfax states that if an incentive program is designed solely around workplace injuries (for example based on xxx months without a claim), the program could come under the scrutiny of OSHA, because it intentionally or unintentionally could discourage the reporting of claims. Just to be clear, OSHA is not opposed to safety incentive programs. Programs designed to promote safety (for example, rewarding employees for their participation in the safety committee or safety related activities, such as safety perception surveys, are strongly encouraged). OSHA's VPP guidance materials refer to positive incentives, including providing tee shirts to workers serving on safety and health committees, offering modest rewards for suggesting ways to strengthen safety and health, or throwing a recognition party at the successful completion of company-wide safety and health training.[24]

COMPOINTS

POSITIVE EMPLOYEES ARE MOTIVATED BY INCENTIVES, BUT NEGATIVE EMPLOYEES RARELY ARE!

Here are some tips for a successful safety motivation program.

Dos

- ☐ Understand the importance of recognition versus reward.

- ☐ Use it to constantly promote your safety program. For example, if you implement a safety perception survey, use an incentive like a safety breakfast for everyone that participates. This is the kind of program OSHA strongly supports!

- ☐ Commit the appropriate time and money to the program. Time (and creativity) will do more than anything to help the program succeed. But creativity requires capital. Give your staff the support they need and your safety motivation program will take flight.

- ☐ Think outside the box. Ask your employees for feedback. I have seen companies use company logo wear, gift cards, even make donations to local nonprofits, and food—which is always a great idea to celebrate and communicate when you hit a safety milestone. There are all kinds of recognition programs you can easily find on the web. For example, Safetybingo.com might be good to utilize in a departmental training or a small company setting. Also, consider small safety tokens that can be given out during safety assessments. A safety token could be anything ranging from a coffee mug or t-shirt all the way to an actually token system (where you give out chips) that can be redeemed for something of value (could be something from the company store or a paid hour off from work). The point of the safety token is small incentives given out on a regular basis. Remember the goal of the safety program is to motivate employees to work safely. Sometimes a simple "job well done" from a supervisor is a valuable prize!

Don'ts

- ☐ Put the focus solely on injuries.
- ☐ Make it complicated.
- ☐ Start with a bang and end with a whimper. This program should be part of your continuous effort to promote safety. If you start the program with a bang and then slowly put it on the back burner, employees might think that safety has been put on the back burner.

Section 2.3.5
Progressive Discipline

COMPOINTS

> IF SUPERVISORS ALLOW UNSAFE BEHAVIOR, IT IS DIFFICULT TO DISCIPLINE EMPLOYEES!

I was raised in an era where there were consequences for your actions. Can you remember those days! Well the workers that are entering today's workforce certainly march to a different drum. We will explore this topic in our chapter on organization, but suffice to say the "do as you're told" mentality doesn't carry the same weight these days! I had five siblings and we operated under Marshal Law. My mom was the Marshal and my dad was the Law! We understood at an early age the importance of following rules and suffering the consequences when we didn't. One of the things I have noticed over the years is the employees who actively participate in the safety process (be it the safety committee, safety training, or even safety motivation programs) are the ones who care about working safely. I think having a progressive discipline program is important, but it is not the cure-all to help establish safety as a core value. The things you include in your progressive discipline policy should include other things like attendance, appearance, and attitude. But as it relates to safety, it should focus on core safety issues that are well defined and that you have included in your training program. More on this in a minute.

There are some considerations if you establish a progressive discipline (PD) program:

- It can be time consuming to manage.

- This could possibly transform an "at will" employee relationship into a contractual one. What this means is if you have a PD program you need to follow it. This may create some rights for the employee (verbal, written warnings, etc.) that you will need to follow instead of simply firing the employee. For example, you make an exception to the at-will status of employees when your policy says, in effect, that they will not be subject to immediate termination for the specific disciplinary infractions included in your progressive discipline policy. Therefore, if absenteeism is one of the disciplinary infractions covered by your progressive discipline policy, you should follow your policy in disciplining an employee for absenteeism unless there are unusual mitigating circumstances.

- Supervisors need to manage all employees the same. Easier said than done! The company may think the written policy is clear. If the enforcement of any policy is random, you are going to have problems.

- When you create a PD program, you run the risk of guaranteeing a process that must be followed. Even if you don't print out the policy and give it to employees, you would be, in effect, telling employees how far they can go. In the event of a challenge, this information can be subpoenaed. Thus, it could be shown in court that your actions differed from your own written policy, which always makes you look bad.

- Documentation is critical. Keep in mind, if you do terminate or use this information in a work comp defense, the information will most likely be produced as evidence. So it is very important to have good records.

Lori Sederditch, editor of Rapid Learning Institute's *Workplace Safety Rapid Learning Center* and blog, summarized safety attorney Adele Abrams' perspective on the pitfalls in establishing a progressive discipline program:[25]

- Special treatment for VIPs

    The obvious: Coming down hard on some people, but not on others. You know treating people the same—regardless of age, race, gender and the like—is essential. Otherwise, you could end up explaining your progressive discipline before the EEOC. But most companies don't pick on people that way.

    The hidden danger: Giving VIPs, important visitors, supervisors, and managers special treatment, and allowing them to violate safety rules.

    Example: The safety director gives a plant tour to VIPs, but doesn't insist they wear seat belts. When a worker is later disciplined for not using a seat belt, she claims that she's been unfairly singled out—and points to the VIP tour as evidence.

    Better: Most managers and supervisors have their own PPE (personal protective equipment), but it's a good idea to make sure they have plenty of spares too. Putting on PPE and delivering a quick safety update (such as wearing seat belts) is an excellent way to create a favorable impression.

- Mishandling complaints

    The obvious: Disciplining after safety complaints. You know that workers who complain about safety enter a legally protected class. Discipline, after that, needs to be handled carefully to avoid even the appearance of retaliation.

    The hidden danger: Allowing safety complaints to undermine progressive discipline. If a worker complains about safety, you need to address it. But that doesn't give the worker a get-out-of-jail free card.

    Example: Bill complains about safety violations, but then repeatedly violates the lockout/tagout policy. His supervisor assumes Bill can't be disciplined. When Bill gets injured, he sues, claiming negligent supervision because his boss failed to enforce the policy.

    Better: A lot depends on how the supervisor handles the discipline, because the worker may be sensitive to anything that looks like retaliation. Start with a discussion—thank the worker for bringing safety concerns up in the past, but then explain that the lockout/tagout policy is for everyone. Just make sure that any changes in policy are clearly communicated (e.g., "We're going to start enforcing tougher policies"), and that the supervisor is not singling the worker out.

- Changing policy by accident

    The obvious: Lack of a progressive discipline policy leaves enforcement up to the individual supervisors, and that's almost guaranteed to result in inconsistent treatment of workers. Most companies think the solution is to write a progressive discipline policy.

The hidden danger: The company thinks the written policy is legally the policy. Actually, your company policy is what your supervisors and workers do on a day-to-day basis.

Example: One company had a written ladder-safety policy. Workers signed statements that they'd read and understood all safety policies and would follow them in their daily jobs. One day, an OSHA inspector found a worker misusing a ladder and issued a fine. The OSHA Review Commission upheld the fine, saying that the company had no evidence it enforced the policies. Without enforcement, the written policy meant nothing, legally.

Better: Review disciplinary records and ask supervisors if these match the actual policy violations. If not, they've accidentally created a new policy.

- Violating procedure

    The obvious: Supervisors don't follow the progressive discipline policy. They make exceptions, ignore violations, or only discipline in severe cases.

    The hidden danger: Supervisors follow the progressive discipline policy as if it were an automatic series of steps. They always warn verbally, then write up, then suspend. This can set up your company for a lawsuit if a worker commits a violation that puts him or her in immediate danger.

    Example: Abrams noted a worker came to work drunk and then hit a fellow worker in a dispute. Should the person be fired or just verbally warned?

    Better: Progressive discipline policies should distinguish between first-offense firings (e.g., lockout violations, threats of violence, or intoxication) and less serious ones.

- Not documenting discipline

    The obvious: Supervisors fail to document discipline. Most companies avoid this risk by requiring documentation of any discipline imposed.

    The hidden danger: Not documenting verbal warnings too. Abrams says she's seen companies get into trouble because supervisors have no record of each other's verbal warnings, so there's no way to be consistent.

    Example: One worker gets several verbal warnings, but nothing happens to him. Another worker, under a different supervisor, is disciplined after one verbal warning. She's in a protected class and files a disparate-treatment lawsuit.

    Better: Supervisors document verbal warnings and you can review them to ensure disciplinary consistency.

I know what you are thinking, this is shaping up to be a lot of work. Unfortunately, you are right, but there are several benefits:

- Employees want a safe work environment. A PD program lets them know the organization has a strong commitment to safety.

- Systematic documentation could give your insurance carrier the necessary information it needs to deny a work comp claim. Several states have statutes that allow the denial of benefits for willful misconduct. Many states include failure to follow safety rules under the definition of willful misconduct. To establish this defense, most attorneys will review your safety training programs and the employee's HR file. Specifically, they will be looking at the employees training record and review your documentation on the employees' adherence to your safety program, which is of course the documentation from your progressive discipline program.

- If you establish an annual performance review process, your progressive discipline policy documentation should answer the performance review questions relating to safety.

COMPOINTS

> YOUR SUPERVISORS MAY BE CALLED TO TESTIFY THAT THEY APPLY PROGRESSIVE DISCIPLINE POLICIES THE SAME FOR ALL EMPLOYEES.

What are some of the things that should be included in the safety portion of your progressive discipline program?

- Anything that is a core part of your safety values. I was at a recent workshop conducted by DuPont. As you probably know, DuPont is one of the leaders in workplace safety. They opened the discussion with an example of their internal programs. They had an employee fall down the stairwell at their office complex. They subsequently instituted a policy where employees have to hold the handrail when they go up or down the stairs. If an employee fails to adhere to this policy, it could result in immediate termination. Now this may seem extreme, but as I discuss in the chapter on organization, their goal is to create a zero accident culture. I would imagine that their aggressive progressive discipline transcends the workplace, and employees take this attitude home with them. WHOA. Imagine that your safety culture was so strong that employees apply this same behavior outside of work!

- You certainly want to include PPE.

- If you are in an industry with mandatory training requirements (i.e., Trench Safety or Arc Flash), you will want to make these items part of your progressive discipline program.

- ☐ Complaints from other workers regarding an employee's unsafe work habits. Be sure to carefully and thoroughly investigate these types of complaints.

Section 2.3.6

Performance Reviews

Do you currently conduct performance reviews? Chances are if you have mostly salary employees you do, and if you have mostly hourly employees you don't. If you don't utilize employee performance reviews, you may want to consider making it part of your workplace safety program. Come again? Part of my workplace safety program? Yes, an effective performance review can help you address and meet the specific needs of each employee. It can also be an opportunity to recognize personal achievement. It can be a great tool to train supervisors and managers, and engage them with their employees. This will facilitate employer-employee communication, and help develop and strengthen relationships.

According to BLR, common objectives of effective performance evaluations are to:

- ☐ Identify a limited number of critical behaviors that are vital to the organization's ability to meet its goals.
- ☐ Enhance employee understanding of the results considered essential to the success of the business.
- ☐ Serve as a tool to determine salary increases based on a worker's contribution to the organization.
- ☐ Give and seek honest feedback because employees perform better when they are allowed to speak openly and clarify performance measures.
- ☐ Apply uniform performance standards that assure fairness and eliminate confusion about performance standards.
- ☐ Give employees a stake in the process by encouraging them to help set their own performance goals and assess their progress in meeting those goals.
- ☐ Make performance management an ongoing process that reflects changes in the business.
- ☐ Gather information for succession planning and the development of training programs by identifying employees who have the interest and potential for advancement.
- ☐ Improve coaching by encouraging supervisors to observe an employee's job performance and compare it with performance standards on an ongoing basis.

So how exactly does this relate to my work comp program? Isn't safety a critical behavior that directly influences the profitability of your company? *Training* teaches the right behavior and *Progressive Discipline* enforces the right behavior, but it is the performance review process that truly enhances the employee's understanding of the results considered essential to the success of the business. I often have employers tell me that the injured employee has taken advantage of the "system." I respond that if you dig deep enough you will probably find clues that this would happen. Another often-heard comment from employers is that we should have terminated the employee long before the work comp claim. But they are stuck, because terminating an employee for employment reasons while they are out of work due to a work related injury will most likely increase the cost of the claim, and in certain conditions, could be considered retaliatory, which could result in fines or penalties.

COMPOINTS

> IT IS USUALLY THE SUBJECTIVE FACTORS, NOT THE OBJECTIVE MEDICAL FACTORS, THAT DRIVE A CLAIM.

I have reviewed tens of thousands of claims in my career. Being an armchair quarterback, I can typically find the red flags (usually hidden but nonetheless present) that influenced the claim. We will discuss this in detail in the section on *Loss*, but the problem with most red flags is they are discovered on a post-claim basis. While they may seem like a smoking gun to you, they usually have limited value in the defense of a workers' compensation claim. I see examples of this quite often. Scan through your own loss history. Pick out the claims where you feel the employee may have taken advantage of the system and ask yourself were there warning signs that could have alerted you a claim was about to happen. In many cases, the answer is yes. At the very least, you will discover information that in the future may help you data mine the employee's HR file to get critical information to the adjuster at the onset of the claim.

A few years ago, I had a client (that was already conducting performance reviews) make the comment that every big claim they experienced involved a person that was "working the system." They were frustrated. In most cases, the employee probably should have been fired due to performance issues—frequently tardy for work, combative to other employees, poor customer service. You probably have employees like this that you allow to continue working. When they get to the point where they sense they are going to be terminated, they file a workers' comp claim. This happened frequently with this particular client, so we piloted a project to drill down into their performance review process. This client had thirty locations. Our goal was to help create an assessment to give us data by location and job position. We wanted to compare the data between the performance reviews and the workers' compensation claims. It was not a surprise to find locations with lower scores on performance reviews were also the locations with the highest frequency and severity of

Process

claims. Was this a function of poor employees or poor managers? In this case, we had some of both. The management took the feedback and focused efforts to improve training and address employees' scores. The next year's results were impressive. Most of the lower performing locations improved their performance scores, and we had a significant reduction in claims! In fact, in the three-year period since we started the pilot, the risk has seen a 27 percent reduction in the experience rating. I am a firm believer that there are many subjective factors that are huge cost drivers in workers' comp claims. Performance reviews may be your most reliable predictive analytics to forecast future work comp claims by helping you address the issue before it manifests itself into a work comp claim.

Here are some tips to help prepare performance reviews.

Step 1: Tweak the process to include safety as part of their review.

Step 2: Limit the criteria to below average, average, and above average.

Step 3: Create training for remediation and recognition for excellence.

Step 4: Create training for the managers that will administer the review.

Step 5: Benchmark the performance reviews against your workers' comp experience.

Step 6: Benchmark results over the previous two or three years to see trends and look for training opportunities.

Section 2.3.7

Supervisor Readiness

COMPOINTS

> SUPERVISORS AREN'T USUALLY SUPERVISORS BECAUSE THEY CAN SUPERVISE. THEY TYPICALLY ARE THE PERSON BEST AT THE JOB; HOWEVER, THAT DOES NOT MAKE THEM LEADERS. A POSITIVE SAFETY CULTURE REQUIRES LEADERSHIP!

I probably broke many grammar rules using "supervise" three times in one sentence in my ComPoint. Up to this point in the comP4 discussion supervisors have been mentioned twenty-three times! This is not random on my part but, in fact, is very intentional because the role of the supervisor in your workplace safety program is critical to the success of the program. They are important because they can make or break your safety credibility. If the supervisor does not lead by example then the employees will not follow. Oftentimes in the life of a workers' comp claim, the supervisors create more problems than solutions! Organizations have to understand that training the supervisor has to be an organizational priority. You cannot expect them to be the torchbearer of your organization's safety culture without training. Consider the example I gave you back in the introduction—the poultry account where I flopped. I did not create a safety program that the supervisor could take out into the plant and make a difference with because they did not have the basic leadership skills to lead the effort. If a supervisor doesn't have leadership skills, they will have a difficult time assimilating comP4. In an article by Stephanie Goddard, she consolidated supervisor mistakes into four categories.[26]

1. Giving feedback based on personality instead of data, behavior, or results.
2. Failing to ensure someone's dignity at the beginning, during, and end of a one-on-one.
3. Not accepting responsibility for every result produced by themselves and their team. Culturally, this is a huge cost driver. The next step in the comP4 process is post-accident. In the post-accident process, we ask the supervisor if the employee was following safety rules. When an accident happens, shouldn't it be a shared responsibility? Certainly, the employee should be held accountable, but shouldn't you also hold the supervisor accountable?
4. Not leading by example. This will swiftly destroy accountability and do long-term damage to your organization's safety culture.

Section 2.3.8

Risk Prevention Services

We have talked about a lot of risk prevention activities, but haven't actually talked about Risk Prevention Consultants. Most employers' experience is with the risk control staff from their insurance company. Typically, their main purpose is to conduct an inspection to determine if you are a safety risk. They take the cursory tour and ask the customary questions. Occasionally, you will get a couple good recommendations and a website full of resources. The best-case scenario is they will provide you some insight to manage the physical hazards associated with your company. But unsafe physical hazards typically only account for 10 percent of all accidents. So risk control visits are usually not productive, and therefore, probably not very high on your to do list. But you can and should change this. Your broker, who knows your business, should help leverage assets from the insurance carrier that can help your organization. Since they probably place many of their clients with a carrier, they should be familiar with their risk control services and the tools they can leverage to help you manage your workplace safety program. Here are some examples:

- ☐ Possible free web-based training
- ☐ A knowledge library to download safety checklists, payroll stuffers, and training material
- ☐ Assistance developing safety assessment forms
- ☐ Assistance on developing an action plan based on accident trends
- ☐ Participation on your safety committee (it is always a good idea to bring in outside speakers to keep the meetings fresh!)
- ☐ Specific training (for example, confined space or forklift safety)
- ☐ Testing and other evaluations (for example, hearing conservation, fit test, and air quality)

To get the most of the risk prevention services offered by an insurance company you (or your broker) have to ask. I also utilize third party risk control if a carrier does not have a service to fit a specific need.

Section 2.3.9

Pre-claim Management Checklist

COMPOINTS

> IF YOUR ORGANIZATION'S PRE-CLAIM CHECKLIST IS NOT FIRMLY IN PLACE BEFORE THE ACCIDENT HAPPENS, YOUR CLAIM WILL BE MORE COSTLY.

Here are some items that should be on your checklist.

Direction to medical:

Have a clear understanding of state-specific requirements for direction to medical.

Postings:

Have all of state-specific postings on the employee bulletin board. If employees work off-site, have documentation stating the employees have seen the postings.

Employee rights and responsibilities:

Some states require employee education regarding their rights and responsibilities. Even if your state does not make this a requirement, it should be part of your new hire process as well as throughout the year, with documentation referencing each instance. In a litigated claim, this documentation will be valuable.

Near misses:

"Near misses" can be defined as minor accidents or close calls that have the potential for property loss or injury. Near misses have been viewed for many years as an aggressive way to address risks in the workplace. According to the National Safety Council, 75 percent of all accidents are preceded by one or more near misses. If employees would recognize these near miss events as potential accidents and take preventive measures, they might avoid more serious and severe outcomes. Reporting of near misses can create an open culture whereby everyone shares and contributes in a responsible manner to their own safety and the safety of fellow employees. Here are some examples of near misses in the workplace:

- An employee trips over an extension cord that lies across the floor, but avoids a fall by grabbing a piece of equipment.
- An employee is walking through a congested production area and narrowly misses being hit by a forklift diving out of the way. The employee dusted himself off and went back to work.
- A ladder is not available and the employee stands on a stack of crates to retrieve an item. The crates give way, but thankfully, the employee was not injured.

Perhaps these types of occurrences are happening throughout your organization. It is not hard to understand the importance of capturing this information as soon as possible to avoid a more severe outcome. Despite the obvious importance, near miss reporting is not widely used. Many employers state it is hard enough to get accidents reported. Even if you implement a near miss program, most organizations have difficulties trending their near misses because of reporting irregularities due to time restraints, fear of discipline, as well as the failure to recognize the importance of such reporting. Here are some tips for developing and implementing a near miss reporting process:

Process

- ☐ **Advertise** – Utilize employee bulletin boards to promote their reporting of near misses to improve the safety culture of your organization. Make the reporting of near misses a topic at all safety meetings and employee newsletters. Talk about it!

- ☐ **Make it easy** – Create an employee safety suggestion box. Provide two-sided cards (bilingual) with "Near Miss" on one side and "Safety Suggestion" on the other. On the "Near Miss" side, the employee would state what happened, where it happened, and how it happened. The "Safety Suggestion" side would provide the employee an opportunity to suggest ways to correct the issue to avoid future incidents. Keep it simple!

- ☐ **Anonymous** – To encourage the reporting of information without fear of disciplinary action, allow the information to be shared anonymously. Mum's the word!

- ☐ **Develop a database** – There are many databases available or you can build a simple database on your own. The benefit of a "pre-built" system is it can easily capture data for statistical analysis, trending, and performance management (improvement over baseline). Know what you know!

- ☐ **Do something with the information** – If you ask for the employees' assistance you must take action when information is provided.

- ☐ **Positive** – If an employee is acting in a reckless manner, you obviously have to take action. But if someone self-reports a near miss, you have to treat this action in a positive manner! Acknowledge the behavior you seek!

Section 2.3.10

Communication

Prevention requires positive communication. Most cars have a small red light and an annoying ding (a subtle reminder) that goes off if you put your car into gear and don't have your seatbelt on. How many times has that happened and you lean over to the passenger and ask them to please put on their seatbelt. This is a great example of a safety communication system. You need to have reminders throughout the workplace to promote and encourage safety.

Here are some examples:

- ☐ **Banners and posters**

- ☐ **Safety signage** – Consider a clock that promotes days without a lost time claim

- ☐ **Safety message on the time clock** – With the advance of web clocks, you can seamlessly tie in a daily or weekly safety message.

- ☐ **Payroll stuffers** – Consider having the back of the payroll stuffer as an entry to a safety incentive drawing. You could take this one-step further by adding language, "During the past thirty days I had a work comp claim and reported it; I had a work comp claim and did not report it; I did not have a work comp claim."

- ☐ **Safety motivation programs** – Remember these should be used to promote (not reward) safety.

- ☐ **Promotion of personal safety** – If you can get employees to think safety outside of work, they are more likely to think safety at work!

- ☐ **Safety suggestion box** – I know this seems old school, but safety suggestion boxes work. If they don't work that probably means you are not positively promoting safety. Keep the box locked and make sure you have suggestion cards available!

Section 2.4
P4 Post-claim

We have discussed a lot of information in steps P1–P3, but P4 is where the rubber meets the road. The efforts you exhaust in P1–P3 will be evident as you go through P4. I have a simple acronym for the post-claim process called **AIM**: the **A**ccident happens, the **I**nvestigation begins, and the claim is **M**anaged.

Section 2.4.1
The Accident Happens

We discussed the importance of near misses in P3 Prevention. Unfortunately, the accident has happened. The accident investigation and management process should be like a tornado drill. You create procedures, you plan and train, and when the event happens you should have confidence that your key players will carry out their roles and stay the course exactly as you expect to ensure a successful outcome. Right? Before we get into the intricacies of the "tornado drill" and the key players involved, let's discuss the potential for loss if any of these key players don't follow the drill.

Process

One of the things we track in our claims management system is lag time. Lag time from when the employee reports the claim, lag time from when the supervisor reports the claim, and finally, the lag time from when the employer reports the claim to the carrier or TPA. Consider the following costs associated with late claims reporting:

- Claims reported within three days cost 15–20% less than claims reported after three days.
- The average cost of a claim increases 3% every day the claim report is delayed.
- Injuries reported two weeks after the date of the accident cost an average of 18% more than those reported during week one.
- Those reported during weeks three and four average a 30% greater cost, and those reported after a month take a whopping 45% increase!
- Litigation is less likely for claims reported immediately. Just 22% of injuries reported within ten days are litigated compared with 47% for those reported after thirty-one days.[27]

Let's talk now about the process of claims reporting to avoid lag time and the costs associated with late claims. I divide claims reporting into **two parts**: the accident report, commonly known as the First Report of Injury, and the accident investigation report, known as the Root Cause Analysis Report—both of which are necessary to file a claim. The First Report of Injury is a short form containing the employee's information and a brief description of the accident. This form should be completed *immediately* to initiate the claim. The Root Cause Analysis Report is the form used to investigate the claim. This form should be completed *within forty-eight hours* of the claim. So, for the purpose of associating these steps with the **AIM** process, the First Report of Injury would fall under **A** and the Root Cause Analysis Report would fall under **I**.

First, let's discuss the key players and their roles. When an accident happens, typically the four parties involved are the employee, the supervisor, the workers' comp coordinator and/or safety person, and the claims adjuster. If you utilize nurse triage that makes five parties. This means there are a lot of hands in the work comp claim. So understanding each party's role is a key factor in creating an accountable workers' compensation program.

The Employee's Role

We talked about the importance of a strong pre-claim communication program as part of P1–P3. Employees need to clearly understand their rights and responsibilities, including the requirement to timely report the claim, thus giving "notice" of the incident. But what constitutes notice? If the employee tells the supervisor, or if the supervisor gains knowledge of an incident, this generally constitutes notice to the employer. If you are a staffing company, notice to your customer may constitute notice to the employer, if your customer is in a supervision capacity.

Here are some considerations:

Do they understand their rights and responsibilities? The two biggest cost drivers are timely reporting and medical claims management.

Why would they delay a claim? One of the most common reasons an employee might delay reporting a claim is because they know they will be drug tested. As we discussed previously, most jurisdictions require that the drug test be performed within a few hours of the accident. Another common reason for late reporting is fear of reprisal from a supervisor.

The Supervisor's Role

I have a simple rule of thumb for supervisors—never let them decide what is, or is not, a reportable claim. Not only will OSHA frown on this (because of supervisor tendency to underreport claims), but late reporting of claims due to supervisor's delay is a leading cost driver for claims. I cannot tell you how many claims go south because of the supervisor's delay in reporting the claim.

Here are some considerations:

Are supervisors trained on how to direct the employee for medical attention? Obviously, if it is an emergency the employee is going to the emergency room, but many claims end up at the emergency room because the employee was not given clear instructions on where to go for medical treatment. That is one of the reasons I like nurse triage services, which we'll discuss a little later. In a panel state like Georgia, where it is the employee's choice from a panel of physicians, educating the supervisors on direction to medical takes on an increased importance.

If you have a second shift or weekend hours, make sure you have a plan for afterhours. I have seen many clients who have a great HR department and a great plan from eight to five, but forget about the afterhours injuries. This is an area that needs to be addressed with your after-hours and weekend shift supervisors.

Do your supervisors show care and concern about the employee? Oftentimes when an employee has an injury and is out of work, their last interaction with your organization may be with the supervisor. If your supervisor does not show genuine care and concern for the injured employee, the employee may feel the *employer* does not care about them.

I realize organization structures vary greatly. If you push the first report down to the supervisor level this could greatly impact the quality of the information sent to your adjuster. Since supervisors don't typically have a high frequency of claims in their department, they are not experienced at completing the accident report. This may be a good reason to consider outsourcing the completion of the first report to a nurse triage service.

The Workers' Comp Coordinator's Role

In most cases, it is the work comp coordinator who submits the First Report of Injury to the insurance carrier or TPA. States differ on direction to medical, so you need to tweak your claims program to reflect your state's requirements. I see a lot of multi-state employers adopt a "one size fits all" strategy. While many of your accident reporting procedures will remain the same, the direction to medical is state-specific. Your broker and/or your insurance carrier/TPA can help you develop these procedures.

The next thing that needs to happen is the claim needs to be immediately reported to the carrier or TPA. Your claims adjuster should conduct a three-point contact (employer, medical provider, and the insured employee) on the claim within twenty-four to forty-eight hours. When claims are taken in by an insurance carrier, they are routed to either a med-only adjuster or a more experienced lost time adjuster, based on the description and/or severity of the claim. Here is an important recommendation. If you have a claim that on paper seems to be a med only, but you know circumstances surrounding the claim could potentially escalate the claim, make sure you note this on your first report. If you don't want to put this information on the first report, call the insurance carrier and get the claim escalated to a lost time adjuster.

Let me give you an example. You have a seemingly small, unwitnessed claim, but you have had someone tell you that the person made comments that they needed off next week and did not have any vacation time left. This is a red flag! When you complete your accident investigation, you may uncover multiple red flags. If you do discover red flags that you feel are material to the claim, you can always request a more experienced lost time adjuster take over the claim.

The Claims Adjuster's Role

Most insurers have two types of adjusters—medical only and lost time. When a claim is submitted at the intake center of an insurer, they review the First Report of Injury and assign the claim based on the accident description.

Medical only adjusters typically handle a huge caseload of claims because the claims are transactional. Their primary responsibility is to ensure the medical bills are paid timely. This makes the recommendation to get a claim escalated, when warranted, to a lost time adjuster even more important.

Lost time adjusters are more experienced adjusters that typically handle an open claim count of around 125 claims. You should always inquire about the desk count of the adjuster. Some insurers, to save money, will overload adjusters. If they have a desk count around 175 they cannot properly manage your claims! This is something you should discuss with your broker.

The Nurse Triage's Role

I mentioned nurse triage earlier. Many organizations are turning to nurse triage companies. The nurse triage takes over the first report responsibility. When an employee is injured, they would call the nurse triage hotline typically while sitting with a supervisor. The intake center would take the first report information, send to your carrier or TPA, and discern if the injury can be treated without going to the doctor by giving advice for self-care. If it's determined the employee needs medical treatment, they will follow the state-specific direction to medical guidelines. This can be a significant cost savings because it will reduce the number of claims requiring medical attention, and more importantly, will reduce the number of emergency room visits. And as I alluded to earlier, an additional benefit to employers is the efficiency and streamlining of this critical first reporting task when being managed by a nurse triage company.

A Quick Guide to Managing an Accident

1. Get the First Report of Injury completed. Who should handle this process?
   a. The Supervisor
      i. Pro
         - They know the most about the employee.
         - They know the most about the jobsite.
      ii. Con
         - They may not be very good at actually completing the report.
   b. The Workers' Comp Coordinator
      i. Pro
         - They are the most knowledgeable person at your company.
      ii. Con
         - They are not always available, and this may delay the report.
         - The employer may have turnover, leaving a void of experience.
   c. The Nurse Triage Company
      i. Pro
         - They are experienced.
         - They can help mitigate self-care cases.
         - They are available 24/7.
         - They can save employers time by taking over the first report responsibility.

Process

      ii. Con
- A nurse triage typically costs between 80–150 dollars per claim depending on the size of the organization and whether you report all incidents or claims only.

2. Ensure that you have state-specific direction to medical.

3. If you have a second shift or weekend workers, make certain you have a strategy and have communicated it to the supervisors working those shifts. Failure to do this could significantly increase your work comp costs!

4. If an employee refuses treatment, have a refusal of treatment form completed.

5. Give the employee an authorization form for medical treatment. Medical providers, and your insurer, appreciate this because it directs them where to bill for the treatment. Many states have penalties if the medical bill is not paid timely, so this ensures the bill goes to the carrier and is not sent to the employer, which could create a delay. An even more problematic scenario would be if the bill were sent to the injured employee. This could drive the injured employee to an attorney.

6. If the employee is transported to the emergency room, you should alert your insurance carrier immediately. In these instances, there may not be time to get an employee statement, but you can request that your insurer dispatch a field adjuster to the hospital to assist you in getting one. Also, an alarming trend with emergency rooms is they will not perform a drug test. The reason is simple. If the test comes back positive, they know your insurer will probably deny the claim, which means they won't get paid. Therefore, it would be a mistake to presume that a drug test will be done at the emergency room! The field adjuster dispatched by your insurance carrier can assist with this as well, so let your expectations be known, and don't leave it to the discretion of the emergency room staff.

7. Emergency room visits are a huge cost driver for claims. If you don't have adequate documentation where you educated the employee about their rights and responsibilities, you might be stuck with the bill three to five times the cost of a traditional office visit.

8. Make sure every effort is made to show care and concern to the injured employee.

C✦MPOINTS

MOST EMERGENCY ROOM VISITS ARE NOT EMERGENCIES.

Section 2.4.2

The Investigation Begins

The claims investigation is typically called the Root Cause Analysis. This should be conducted on every accident. Yes, even the "med only" claims. Why? A med only claim may escalate into a "lost time" claim. Also, by conducting a Root Cause Analysis on every claim you will improve your investigation process, and the information gathered in the process is a great discussion point for your safety meetings. The Root Cause Analysis should contain four sections: the employee statement, the supervisor statement, a witness statement, and the employer review. You should customize these questions to fit your organization. For example, a decentralized organization that pushes more of the responsibility to the field office will push more of the questions over to the supervisors. A centralized operation will push more questions onto the claims coordinator. The Root Cause Analysis form should ask for a statement of what happened and should ask "root cause" questions. Here are some best practices:

- ☐ **Employee** – Make certain the employee fully completes, and signs, the form. The best time to get the unfiltered facts from an employee is immediately after the accident happens. Any delay could result in material changes to the employee's statement. If the employee cannot read the form, have someone attest that they explained the form and have that person sign the form. Have the forms translated if you have a non-English speaking workforce.

    Sample root cause questions:

    1. Could you have prevented the injury? Yes ☐ No ☐
    2. Were you following the company's safety rules? Yes ☐ No ☐
    3. Did you have any medical conditions at the time of the accident? Yes ☐ No ☐

COMPOINTS

> IF SUPERVISORS AREN'T TRAINED ON ACCIDENT INVESTIGATIONS, IT WILL REFLECT IN THE QUALITY OF THE INFORMATION REPORTED AND THE COST OF THE CLAIM!

Process

- **Supervisor** – The supervisor's report is one of the most critical pieces of a best in class claims management program; therefore, you must hold the supervisor accountable for completing their portion of the accident investigation. Consideration should be given to conducting a supervisor accident investigation training on an annual basis. Because supervisor positions change frequently, I have developed a web-based training module for my clients. This way the management team can assign and track who has completed the training, and how often. If you don't have a learning management system, you can create the training in a slide presentation and develop a paper quiz to assess the supervisor's understanding of your accident investigation process.

    Sample root cause questions:

    1. Could anything be done to prevent this type of accident in the future? Yes ☐ No ☐
       If **yes**, please explain._____
    2. Was the employee following safety rules? Yes ☐ No ☐
       If **no**, please explain._____
    3. Was someone else involved in the accident? Yes ☐ No ☐
       If **yes**, please explain._____
    4. Was horseplay, negligence, or criminal activity present? Yes ☐ No ☐
       If **yes**, please explain._____
    5. Did anything in the workplace contribute to the accident? Yes ☐ No ☐
       If **yes**, please explain._____
    6. Did you report the claim as soon as you had notice? Yes ☐ No ☐
       If **no**, please explain._____
    7. Did the employee have the proper training for their job? Yes ☐ No ☐
       If **no**, please explain._____
    8. Has the employee expressed any displeasure with their job? Yes ☐ No ☐
       If **yes**, please explain._____

- **Witness** – The witness is also an important part of the accident investigation. Just like the employee statement, is important to get the witness statement at the time of the accident. By the time the claim goes into litigation, the witness might not still be your employee or may change their story.

Sample root cause questions:

1. Was the employee working safely? Yes ☐ No ☐

   If **no**, please explain._____

2. Did the employee mention any previous medical conditions? Yes ☐ No ☐

   If **yes**, please explain._____

3. Do you know if the employee works somewhere else? Yes ☐ No ☐

   If **yes**, please explain._____

4. How long have you known the employee? _____

☐ **Employer** – The employer recap is for the workers' comp coordinator to complete. This information will be invaluable to the adjuster to help them develop an action plan for the claim.

Sample root cause questions:

1. Were there conflicting descriptions of what happened? Yes ☐ No ☐

   If **yes**, please explain._____

2. Was there a safety violation? Yes ☐ No ☐

   If **yes**, was there disciplinary action taken? Yes ☐ No ☐

   If **yes**, list disciplinary action._____

3. Did employee have any health concerns that may have contributed? Yes ☐ No ☐

   If **yes**, please explain._____

4. Has this employee had a history of injuries? Yes ☐ No ☐

   If **yes**, please explain._____

5. Was a post-injury drug/alcohol test given? Yes ☐ No ☐

   If **yes**, was the test positive? Yes ☐ No ☐

   If **no**, did the employee refuse to take a drug/alcohol test? Yes ☐ No ☐

6. Was the job being eliminated? Yes ☐ No ☐

7. Was there anything noted on the health history questionnaire? Yes ☐ No ☐

   If **yes**, please explain._____

8. Has the employee had previous workers' compensation claims? Yes ☐ No ☐

   If **yes**, please explain._____

9. Did the employee delay reporting? Yes ☐ No ☐

   If **yes**, please explain._____

10. Does the employee work somewhere else? Yes ☐ No ☐

    If **yes**, please explain._____

11. Could the employee have been injured away from work? Yes ☐ No ☐

    If **yes**, please explain._____

12. Is there a history of disciplinary actions with the employee? Yes ☐ No ☐

    If **yes**, please explain._____

Section 2.4.3

The Claim is Managed

Managing a workers' comp claim is difficult because there are so many variables. Very few claims are exactly alike; however, there are some fundamentals to apply for every claim.

- ☐ Show care and concern throughout the whole claim, not just at the onset of the claim.

- ☐ Make sure the medical is being managed. To do this you first must follow your state specific guidelines on direction to medical. Next, if you are in a state that allows you to choose the doctor, be sure to utilize quality doctors.

- ☐ Manage the return to work (RTW). Unless it is a medical necessity for an employee to be out of work, don't ever let them sit at home drawing a check. You must be vigilant on this. If an employee ever develops the mindset that they can stay out of work and still receive a paycheck, they may decide they really do not want to return to work. I had an attorney refer to this as "negative charisma." If an employee develops "negative charisma," you have a difficult, time-consuming, and potentially expensive case. The longer the employee is out of work, the less likely they are to ever return to work.

C✦MPOINTS

ODDS OF RETURNING TO WORK

LENGTH OF TIME OUT OF WORK	ODDS OF RTW
6 MONTHS	50%
1 YEAR	25%
2 YEARS	<2%

Tips to manage RTW:

- Make sure the authorized treating physician has the regular job description and understands that you will attempt to accommodate the injured employee with a transitional position.

- Transitional position does not mean you have to create a new job. Here are some options for transitional duty:
    - Modify original duties
    - Modify original job schedule – Most jurisdictions have a provision to pay employees work comp benefits if you bring them back less hours or at less pay. It is a good idea to consider bringing someone back to graduated duty if they have been out for an extended period with an injury. This is called "work hardening." It is respectful to the employee and significantly reduces the likelihood that the employee will go back out of work.
    - Provide assistance doing original job
    - Offer another job that fits restrictions
    - Create a transitional job within restrictions
    - Partner with a nonprofit – Many states will allow the placement of injured employees at a nonprofit (for example, The Red Cross to stuff envelopes).
    - Utilize a RTW company to assist you in placement – Your broker can recommend a third party vendor that can provide this service. The cost is around $850 per claim. One national vendor touts these stats on their website:

- 92% of injured worker's benefits were ended within one week of referral
- 94% placement success rate
- Reduced average indemnity claim by twenty-eight days
- Transitional duty assignments located within one to seven business days
- Assignments usually end within ninety days

☐ Track the days away from work and communicate with your adjuster. Oftentimes neither party knows the employee's work status. This is a big cost driver.

☐ If you manage an OSHA log, map your claims file to your OSHA log. The two should be in sync. The best practice is to keep your claim and your OSHA log in sync by using software to manage both processes with one tool. Many claims portals will allow you to do that. If you do not have access to an online claims portal make sure you reconcile your claim lost time with your OSHA lost days. Please remember your claim's lost days are counted by the actual days away from work and OSHA counts lost work days on a calendar basis. For example, a week away from work might be five workdays (for a WC claim) but would be seven calendar days (on OSHA log). More on this in the chapter on loss.

Action Plans

Once I develop the actual claims reporting process for my clients, my next step is to develop an action plan. The action is a "To Do" checklist of things that should be done on a claim. I utilize a 3/7/21-day action plan. Here is a sample plan.

3-Day Plan (automatic)

1. Did the employee follow proper direction to medical? Yes ☐ No ☐
2. Was the accident investigation form completed? Yes ☐ No ☐
3. Did the employee return to their regular job? Yes ☐ No ☐
4. Were there any root cause exceptions? (listed below – auto generated)
5. Should the claim be closed? Yes ☐ No ☐

   If **no**, do you want to activate action plan? Yes ☐ No ☐

7-Day Plan – Employer

The following will be sent to carrier/TPA within seven days for all claims that have compensability issues or are lost time claims.

1. Accident investigation form
2. Post-offer health questionnaire
3. Direction to medical care
4. Wage statement
5. Medical release form
6. Regular job Description

21-Day Plan – Carrier/TPA

On all claims with compensability and/or are lost time claims, employer will receive a compensability report with the following items on or before the twenty-first day.

1. Review claim for compensability
2. Review medical notes for compensability and cross reference with post-offer heath questionnaire
3. Send ATP job description
4. Do database searches (ISO, Factel, Trace)
5. Notify client regarding acceptance or denial

The three-day action plan should be on every claim. You should have a three-day follow-up to review these items on a claim. If the claim looks like it is going to be a lost time claim, you should initiate the seven- and twenty-one-day action plans. Let me explain why these timings are so important. In many jurisdictions, the insurer/TPA only has a limited time (typically twenty-one days) to investigate the claim for compensability and commence benefits. Therefore, they need all the information from you on a timely basis to determine compensability.

I have seen numerous claims where important "smoking gun" information comes out three months into the claim, and the value of this information may be diluted because it was not given to the adjuster on a timely basis. Without giving a legal exposé, there is a burden on the insurer/TPA to investigate a claim within the statutory period (for example, twenty-one days in Georgia). If the employer should have made information available but failed to do so, it might be inadmissible later, or the value of the information could be diluted. You should also have your carrier/TPA timely communicate the action plan back to you. Every carrier and TPA has internal standards, which include developing an action plan in xxx (typically twenty-one) amount of days. While they may be doing this internally, oftentimes they forget to communicate what they

Process

have done on a file with the insured. Therefore, you should set an expectation that you will be looking for this information and set a reminder to ensure the adjuster sends you this information. This will prevent your claim from getting lost in the shuffle.

Performance Standards

All brokers (myself included) promise lower claims costs. But we all take different paths. Like most brokers, I focus on Total Cost of Risk (TCOR), but sometimes bad stuff happens to great organizations. Therefore, I like to put most of my focus on performance standards. For example, if I set up the 3/7/21-day action plan we described above, I want to monitor whether the client and the adjuster are meeting those deadlines. My goal is lowest costs, and to achieve that goal, I want to make sure everyone is doing all they can to manage the cost. You don't need a fancy system like my Compass RMS to measure performance standards. You could simply create an electronic spreadsheet to track the action plan items. You can get most of the information listed below from the insurance carrier loss run (a loss run is the list of losses from your insurance carrier).

Because there is a tremendous amount of leakage in workers' compensation, here are additional performance standards you should consider:

- ☐ Lag time (employee/supervisor/claim coordinator)
- ☐ Direction to medical (percent of claims)
- ☐ Litigated claims
- ☐ Lost time claims
- ☐ Days Away, Restricted, and Transferred (DART) rate and OSHA calculation discussed in the chapter on loss
- ☐ Nature of injury[*]
- ☐ Body part

Dedicated Adjusters

If you have more than twelve lost time claims a year in a specific state, you should request a dedicated adjuster. Communication is extremely important, so if you can develop a rapport with an adjuster it will give you a tremendous amount of traction on your claims. Please note that if you have

---

[*] Some companies use cause or nature of injury trend as a performance standard in their targeted safety initiative.

the same twelve lost time claims across multiple jurisdictions you probably will not get a dedicated adjuster because adjusters are usually state specific.

Dedicated Legal Counsel

IF YOU HAVE THE SAME LEGAL COUNSEL ON EVERY CLAIM, THEY WILL BE VERY INTIMATE WITH YOUR ORGANIZATION'S SAFETY CULTURE.

If you have a dedicated adjuster, you have enough claims volume to ask for dedicated legal counsel. For the same reasons mentioned above, having legal counsel familiar with your organization is very important. To adequately represent you on a claim they are probably going to have to familiarize themselves with all of your HR and safety polices. That takes time! So, if you have the same counsel they are in a position to represent you better and their bill will be less. Another benefit of having dedicated counsel is they probably will provide free training on changes in the law, and might even give you some pro bono work if you have a question.

Claim Reviews

My feeling about claims reviews are mixed. For the most part, it is not the best use of time. Oftentimes your broker wants to beat up the adjuster to make them feel like they are your advocate. In my opinion, the claim review process should happen 24/7. That is why I put so much emphasis on claims coordinator training, action plans, and performance standards. Claims reviews are a good tool to build relationships, strategize on a specific claim, and discuss the overall relationship. But the claim review process typically works like this: a couple days before the review someone from the brokers' office calls the adjuster to get up to speed on the claims so they can be relevant at the claim review. To the adjuster who is on top of his or her files, this can be a very frustrating exercise. I also have seen where the claim review can become combative because of posturing in front of the decision maker. Please don't mistake my comments. Claims reviews are necessary, but the goal should be to build closer relationships, discuss performance standards, and map out strategies on difficult claims.

Process

Tips for an effective claim review:

- ☐ Take good notes so you will be able to track progress between reviews.
- ☐ Have a call to action for each claim. I can remember sitting in a staff meeting with a small boutique work comp carrier (who was gobbled up by a large insurer), and they would discuss every open claim over a certain size in their weekly staff meeting. This took time, but you want to talk about accountability. They did not allow claims to get too far off track. The manager kept really good notes to track progress (on the call to action).
- ☐ Look for training opportunities. Oftentimes, claim reviews focus on specific claims but if you focus on trends it may help you develop strategies to mitigate future claims.
- ☐ Discuss performance standards.

In closing, I have covered a lot of ground in my comP4 process and you may be feeling a little overwhelmed. I started the book by saying less is more! Pick out the parts of this process that will produce the most impact for your organization. Remember your broker can help you create a long-term plan that will help guide you through this process.

---

[1] "More than Two-Thirds of Businesses Affected by a Bad Hire in the Past Year, According to CareerBuilder Survey Headline," CareerBuilder press release, December 8, 2011, http://www.pitchengine.com/careerbuilder/more-than-twothirds-of-businesses-affected-by-a-bad-hire-in-the-past-year-according-to-careerbuilder-surveyheadline.

[2] "Nearly Seven in Ten Businesses Affected by a Bad Hire in the Past Year, According to CareerBuilder Survey," CareerBuilder press release, December 13, 2012. http://www.careerbuilder.com/share/aboutus/pressreleasesdetail.aspx?sd=12/13/2012&sc_cmp1=cb_pr730_&siteid=cbpr&id=pr730&ed=12/31/2012.

[3] Celina Oliver et al., "Use of Integrity Tests May Reduce Workers' Compensation Losses," *Faculty Scholarship (SPP)*, Paper 8 (2011), http://commons.pacificu.edu/sppfac/8/.

[4] Michael C. Sturman and David Sherwyn, "The Truth About Integrity Tests: The Validity and Utility of Integrity Testing for the Hospitality Industry," *Cornell Hospitality Reports* 7, no. 15 (2009), https://www.hotelschool.cornell.edu/research/chr/pubs/reports/abstract-14602.html.

[5] Stephenie Overman, "Tools and Techniques: Don't be a Target," *Staffing Management Magazine* 4, no. 2 (2008), quoted in Susan M. Grant, "How to Spot Problems on Employment Applications," *eHow*, http://www.ehow.com/how_5666025_spot-problems-employment-applications.html.

[6] "Application Forms: What You Can Ask," Business and Legal Resources, website, October 15, 2002, http://hr.blr.com/whitepapers/Staffing-Training/Application-Forms/Application-Forms-What-You-Can-Ask.

[7] 42 U.S.C. § 12111.

[8] "Drug-free Workplace Resources," National Institute of Drug Abuse, last modified July 2008, http://www.drugabuse.gov/related-topics/drug-testing/drug-free-workplace-resources.

[9] *Report to the Nations: On Occupational Fraud and Abuse*, Association of Certified Fraud Examiners (2012): 17.

[10] *Id.*, 13.

[11] Joseph T. Wells, "Protect Small Business," *Journal of Accountancy* (March 2003), http://www.journalofaccountancy.com/Issues/2003/Mar/ProtectSmallBusiness.htm.

[12] 29 CFR §1630.14(b).

[13] 29 CFR §1630.14(b)(3).

[14] *A Technical Assistance Manual on the Employment Provisions (Title I) of the Americans with Disabilities Act*, §6.1 (1992).

[15] 29 CFR §1630.14(b)(1).

[16] 29 CFR §1630.14(c).

[17] *EEOC Enforcement Guidance: Workers' Compensation and the ADA* (1996).

[18] 29 CFR §1630, *Appendix-Interpretative Guidance on Title I on the Americans with Disabilities Act*.

[19] 29 CFR, *Appendix to Part 1630 - Interpretative Guidance on Title I of the Americans with Disabilities Act*, §1630.14(c).

[20] *EEOC Technical Assistance Manual*, Section 4.4.

[21] 29 CFR §1630.10.

[22] Norman Root, "Injuries at work are fewer among older employees," *Monthly Labor Review* (March 1981), http://www.bls.gov/opub/mlr/1981/03/art4full.pdf.

[23] Richard E. Fairfax, Deputy Assistant Secretary, US Department of Labor, "Employer Safety Incentive and Disincentive Policies and Practices," March 12, 2012, https://www.osha.gov/as/opa/whistleblowermemo.html.

[24] *See* "Revised Policy Memo #5 - Further Improvements to VPP" (June 29, 2011).

[25] Lori Sederditch, "Discipline: 5 ways you can get in legal trouble," *RapidLearning Institute*, blog, http://rapidlearninginstitute.com/workplace-safety/discipline-legal-trouble.

[26] Stephanie Goddard, "The Four Biggest Mistakes a Supervisor Can Make," *The Call Centre*, website, http://www.callcentres.com.au/reonj.htm.

[27] "Report the Claim—and Save Right from the Start," *COMPress* (April 2009), https://www.summitholdings.com/wc/PageReader/employers/publications/comppress/files/comppress4-09.pdf.

Chapter 3
Loss

> There's always failure. And there's always disappointment. And there's always loss. But the secret is learning from the loss, and realizing that none of those holes are vacuums.
>
> – Michael J. Fox

Ben Franklin said that death and taxes are the only two certainties in life; however, I'd like to add a third certainty—Loss. Organizations see and feel the impact of Loss every day, but very few truly *understand* the impact Loss has on their organization. This chapter is designed to increase your understanding of the total cost of risk (Loss) and to share with you ways to minimize your exposure through proven strategies. To be clear, my references to Loss are specific to those associated with workers' compensation. If I expanded this book to include all organizational risk, it would probably cause a work comp injury just lifting it!

In this chapter, we'll discuss Total Cost of Risk, Analyzing Loss Runs, Experience Rating and Classifications, and Claims IQ. If you would like to gain a better understanding of the emerging risks your organization faces, I would suggest you review the RIMS (The Risk Management Society) annual benchmarking survey at www.rims.org.

Section 3.1

Total Cost of Risk - TCOR

No discussion of TCOR would be complete without the iceberg graphic. This is a great illustration to help draw the attention to the "hidden," indirect costs associated with a claim. It is proven these indirect costs are typically three to five times (OSHA says four and a half times) that of direct costs, so why don't more organizations pay attention to indirect costs?[1] One of the reasons is most brokers only focus on activities that drive the direct costs. They will shop your business for the best price, and may try to get claims closed to help you get lower rates on your renewal. This is a price strategy, not a cost strategy. The encouraging news is that this is improving. According to a survey commissioned by Wausau Insurance Company (Wausau Multiline Productivity Poll surveyed 200 financial executives), 71 percent of the respondents said their agent or broker "always or usually" counsels them on TCOR.

With more brokers embracing the TCOR lingo, how can you differentiate the message? If your broker has a TCOR discussion with you, it is usually limited to direct and indirect costs. Preventative costs are seldom addressed during discussions on TCOR. This is a missed opportunity! The investment you make in prevention will have a huge impact on your TCOR. According to the Department of Labor, each dollar of investment by an employer in a health and safety plan can save the company four to six dollars. That is a pretty impressive return on your investment! This led me to add "in the clouds" to my version of the traditional iceberg illustration. I'll explain. Icebergs form from glaciers that break off and go out into the sea. Glaciers are formed when snow accumulates and freezes more rapidly than it can melt. There would be no glaciers if there was no snow and snow originates in the clouds. Therefore, if you want to impact the iceberg, you have to start where it all began—in the clouds. Although this is a different twist to what you will read in any book on TCOR, it is my grounded philosophy that if you want to impact your TCOR you have to invest in prevention.

C✦MPOINTS

IF YOU ONLY ADDRESS DIRECT AND INDIRECT COSTS ASSOCIATED WITH A LOSS, YOU ARE LEAVNG OUT AN IMPORTANT ELEMENT IN THE TCOR EQUATION.

Section 3.1.1

Preventative Costs (In the Clouds)

The following items would be considered preventative:

- Pre-Employee Screening – As previously discussed, integrity testing is a proven way to reduce direct and indirect costs.

- Safety Equipment – Having the right hardware (safety equipment) in place helps create a safety culture mentality.

- Culture Management – I break an organization's safety culture down into two categories: Claims IQ and Safety IQ.

- Wellness – Wellness has been the buzz for many years. We know successful wellness programs lead to fewer workers' compensation claims, so why don't more organizations focus on wellness? This is a strategic focus of mine, and I will delve deeper into this subject on my website: www.managedcomp.net.

- New Hire Training – The tone for the safety culture has to be set in the new hire safety orientation.

- Salary of Safety Personnel and Expenses – If you don't invest in an adequate infrastructure, safety will not be first in your organization (maybe not even second or third).

- Safety Meetings – Based around a meeting agenda for effective use of employees' time away from productivity.

- Contributions to a Safety Motivation Program – It is a proven, sound business strategy to invest in your employees.

- Personal Protective Equipment (PPE) – In many cases, OSHA requires PPE. You should spend a little extra effort exceeding the minimum requirements. For example, I had a metal fabricator who had a high incidence of eye injuries. Thankfully, they were small claims, but we knew if this exposure continued we were going to have a catastrophic claim. The client provided the protective glasses (per OSHA regs), and tried to enforce compliance. During an employee safety luncheon, we polled the employees to find out why so many employees were having eye injuries. The safety consultant had a really fancy pair of safety glasses and offered them to the first person who would volunteer why they didn't wear their safety glasses. A slew of hands went up. What we discovered is the inexpensive glasses the employer was providing impeded the employee's production, so they would typically take them off. Supervisors were lax on enforcement because they had tight production deadlines. When we heard the feedback, the client contracted with a company to provide fit testing and increased their expenditures to provide better safety glasses. Compliance went up and claims went down almost immediately.

Sometimes the solutions are not that complicated. If you simply ask the employees what they think, they will generally tell you. But be careful what you ask. If you ask them for suggestions to improve safety, you should always respond to their requests. It doesn't mean you can always accommodate their requests, but if you want to maintain the dialogue with your employees, you need to respond. I have seen employers that will have safety suggestion boxes, but never respond to the suggestions. It doesn't take long before the suggestions stop because the employees feel that management doesn't care about them. This actually can drive up losses!

In 2007, OSHA issued a new rule about employer payment for PPE. The standard makes clear that employers cannot require workers to provide their own PPE, and the worker's use of PPE they already own must be completely voluntary.[2] Even when a worker provides his or her own PPE, the employer must ensure the equipment is adequate to protect the worker from hazards at the workplace. Examples of PPE that the employer must pay for include:

- Metatarsal foot protection
- Rubber boots with steel toes
- Non-prescription eyewear
- Prescription eyewear inserts/lens for full face respirators
- Goggles and face shields
- Firefighting PPE
- Hard hats
- Hearing protection
- Welding PPE

Payment exceptions under the rule:

- Non-specialty, safety-toe protective footwear (including steel-toe boots) and non-specialty prescription safety eyewear provided the employer permits such items to be worn off the job site. (OSHA based this decision on the fact that this type of equipment is very personal, is often used outside the workplace, and is taken by workers from jobsite to jobsite and employer to employer.)

- Everyday clothing, such as long sleeve shirts or long pants, street shoes, and normal work boots.

- Ordinary clothing, skin creams, or other items used solely for protection from weather, such as winter coats, jackets, gloves, parkas, rubber boots, hats, raincoats, ordinary sun glasses, and sunscreen.

- Items such as hairnets and gloves worn by workers for consumer safety.

- Lifting belts because their value in protecting the back is questionable.

- When the employee has lost or intentionally damaged the PPE and it must be replaced.

Section 3.1.2

Direct Costs (Above the Water)

The following items are considered direct losses:

- Premiums paid
- Claims*
    - Medical – This is the amount paid for medical benefits (according to NCCI, this constitutes 59% of the claim).
    - Indemnity – This is the benefit associated with wage replacement (41% of the claim).
    - TTD (Temporary Total Disability) – When the employee is totally out of work.
    - TPD (Temporary Partial Disability) – When the employee is back at work in a transitional capacity.
    - PPD (Permanent Partial Disability) – Paid when an impairment rating is given by the authorized treating physician.

---

* A great resource to look up your state's benefits is www.claimwire.com.

- LAE (Loss Adjustment Expenses) – These are also called allocated costs, and can be costs for things like attorney fees or private investigators. Some insurers may also include a charge for fee schedule reductions as part of LAE.
- Deductibles or retentions

How are claims valued?

$$\text{Paid} + \text{Reserved} = \text{Incurred} + \text{IBNR} = \text{Carrier's Loss Ratio}$$

It is very important to understand this formula. Most employers understand what incurred claims are but fail to understand the impact of IBNR (incurred but not reported). IBNR is an estimate of the amount of insurer's liability for claim-generating events that have taken place but not yet reported to the insurer. Every insurance carrier loads in a percentage for IBNR. Why is this so important? Well, insurers underwrite to a certain loss ratio, and that loss ratio includes IBNR. When investment income is high, they can write to a higher loss ratio because of the long tail on work comp claims. Long tail? In workers' comp claims, insurers know big claims are paid out over many years (hence the term "long tail"), and they have your premium and are collecting investment income on that dollar. But with interest rates at historic lows, insurance carriers are trying to make an underwriting profit. That means if they collect a dollar from you they want to have claims and expenses less than a dollar. With expenses running around 37 percent (things like underwriting, claims, risk control, and brokers' commissions), that leaves 63 percent for claims to be a break-even customer. And that 63 percent does not include IBNR! Insurers are not looking for breakeven customers! Because medical, indemnity, and legal costs are all up and investment income is at historic lows, you are seeing increased pressure to raise work comp rates.

Section 3.1.3

Indirect Costs (Below the Water)

- Damage to equipment, machinery, materials, facility, etc.
- Production downtime
- Lower employee morale
- Loss of products or services

- ☐ Loss of customers
- ☐ Delays in shipment or filling orders
- ☐ Additional overtime
- ☐ Managers' lost time resulting from the accident—includes inspections, investigations, meetings, and administration
- ☐ Employees assisting with the accident—includes administering first aid, and witness interviews
- ☐ Hiring and training replacement workers
- ☐ Wages of replacement workers
- ☐ Other non-productive time incurred by the injured employee—includes all medical-related appointments
- ☐ Potential OSHA penalties
- ☐ Attorney fees
- ☐ Damage to reputation

Section 3.1.4
Calculating TCOR

For TCOR to have any lasting impact on your organization, it must be measured. This can be very difficult in smaller organizations. If your organization purchases business interruption insurance, you probably complete a business interruption worksheet. This worksheet carefully analyses your continuing expenses and your loss of profit should you have a property claim. It is a "what if" exercise you complete each year. The TCOR calculation is very similar. It is a thought process to analyze your costs associated with prevention and loss, both direct and indirect. One word of caution. Managing your TCOR is not a short-term proposition. Investments in prevention don't always yield immediate benefits; however, if you perform a TCOR calculation year in and year out, you will begin to gain quantifiable results. Your broker should have a TCOR worksheet he can give you. You can find a great (simple) TCOR calculator by going to the OSHA website—www.osha.gov—and typing "safety pays calculator" in the search window. Since the discussion of TCOR should include prevention, be sure and talk about this with your broker. They are your outsourced risk manager, and would welcome the opportunity to help you go through this exercise.

Loss

Section 3.2
Analyzing a Loss Run

You need to get a loss run more than once a year. I suggest if you have *less than* six lost time claims a year, semi-annual loss runs will probably suffice. However, if you have *more than* six lost time claims a year, you should be getting your claims on a monthly basis. If you have *twelve or more* lost time claims a year, you should get your loss run monthly and have a loss trending report at least quarterly. This trending report will help you focus your risk management efforts. Almost every carrier can give you this detail, and your trending report should include:

- ☐ Lag time
- ☐ Day of the week
- ☐ Time of day
- ☐ Percent of litigated claims
- ☐ By nature of injury
- ☐ By body part
- ☐ By department

Timing of when you review loss runs can have a huge impact on your experience rating mod, which we will discussed next. Also, losses should be evaluated every month as part of your safety committee meetings.

Section 3.3
Experience Rating and Classifications

There are few things pertaining to work comp that can be as confusing or misunderstood as your experience rating worksheet (commonly referred to as your experience mod or x-mod) and how your account is classified. When I first started on the agency side over thirty years ago, I knew very little about the experience rating mod. I was told the mod was the mod and everybody had to use it as part of their rate making. Well that is true and false. It is true that if a mod is correctly calculated it does apply to all carriers competing for your business. But no one seemed to pay any attention to the data that was being submitted to promulgate your mod, nor were agencies very proactive in helping clients manage claims to mitigate future mods. Well, those days have changed. Nearly every agency has access to an experience rating software program to analyze your mod. I use a product by Zywave called ModMaster. It is a great tool to analyze data and generate meaningful reports to help your organization understand the cost of claims.

Section 3.3.1
What Is an Experience Rating?

A simple explanation is NCCI receives claims and payroll data from your insurance carrier(s), and based on the data they collect for all employees, they calculate whether you are better (credit mod) or worse (debit mod) than average (1.00 mod). If you are new in business, it may take you up to four years to earn your first mod. Here are the common questions I get from employers regarding the experience rating mod.

Section 3.3.2
What Time Period Do They Use?

The x-mod typically looks at a three-year period of claims. The formula does not include the latest year and uses the three prior years, and can go back further if you have changed effective dates during the four-year period.

COMPOINTS

> YOU SHOULD ALWAYS ANALYZE CLAIMS MORE THAN SIX MONTHS BEFORE YOUR RENEWAL DATE TO MAKE SURE THEY ARE CORRECTLY REPORTED TO THE RATING BUREAU.

Loss

Most states use NCCI as the rating bureau, but even when NCCI is the bureau, the rating rules can be state specific. The claims that go on the experience rating worksheet are typically valued six months before your anniversary or rating effective date. This is usually your renewal date, unless you have had some midterm changes in your annual renewal date and it could take a year or so for the mod anniversary date to match up with your renewal date.

Section 3.3.3

What Are the Factors on the Mod Worksheet?

Even though most of the factors are outside of your control, it is important for you to understand the rating factors. There are five factors that impact your mod:

Class code (column 1):

You will always want to make certain they are using the correct class codes and audited payrolls (column 2).

Payroll (column 4)

Injury Code (column 8):

This is extremely important if you are in an ERA state.

IJ Code Medical Claim	
IJ Code 1	Death
IJ Code 2	Permanent Total Disability
IJ Code 5	Temporary Total or Temporary Partial Disability
IJ Code 6	Medical-Only
IJ Code 7	Contract Medical or Hospital Allowance
IJ Code 9	Permanent Partial Disability

"W" factor

The value keyed on expected losses is calculated on a state-by-state basis. If you are a multi-state risk then you will get a weighted average. This value is multiplied by your excess losses (the amount over the split point).

Split Point

NCCI adopted the new split point in 2013 in all thirty-four NCCI states plus the District of Columbia. The independent rating bureaus in Indiana, Michigan, Minnesota, New York, North Carolina, and Wisconsin also adopted the change. Other independent states may consider it as well, so you should ask your broker if the split point applies to you. Chances are you have already had this conversation, as the revised split point could have a huge impact on your work comp costs.

In experience rating, each loss is divided into a primary and excess portion. The split point refers to how much of the claim will be considered primary. Up until the change in the split point, the amount was $5,000. Per NCCI:

> The $5,000 split point has not changed for approximately twenty years. During this time, the Plan has seen the average dollar amount per claim approximately triple. Because of this, the portion of each claim that flows into the experience rating formula at full value (primary loss amount) is much smaller than what it used to be twenty years ago. The result is that the Plan is giving less weight to each employer's actual experience. Consequently, the Plan formula has become less responsive, and individual employer experience rating modifications have gravitated toward the all-risk average over time.[3]

The split point will increase as follows: 2013 – 10,000; 2014 – 13,500; 2015 – 15,000; and 2016 and after indexed for inflation.

So how exactly will this impact your company? Earlier I told you that a loss is divided into two parts. The primary loss and the excess loss. The experience rating calculation takes 100 percent of the primary loss and a percentage of the excess. This percentage of the excess is listed at the bottom of your mod worksheet and is noted as the "w" value.

Loss

1	2	3	4	5	6	7		8	9	10	11
CODE	ELR	D-RATIO	PAYROLL	EXPECTED LOSSES	EXP.PRIM LOSSES	CLAIM DATA #	ID	IJ	POLICY DATE	ACT. INC. LOSSES	ACT. PRIM. LOSSES
				(D) - (E)		(H) - (I)					
	0.45		1,845,290	2,330,366	485,076	526,943			252,650	694,066	167,123
	"W" VALUE		EXPECTED EXCESS	TOTAL EXPECTED	TOTAL EXP. PRIM.	ACTUAL EXCESS			"B" VALUE	TOTAL ACTUAL	TOTAL ACT. PRIM.
	A	B	C	D	E	F			G	H	I

				11	12	13	14	
# Limited loss.			Experience Modification Calculation	PRIMARY LOSSES	STABILIZING VALUE	RATABLE EXCESS	ADJUSTED TOTALS	
S Subrogation or other special loss.								15
	16		ACTUAL	(I)	(C) X (1-W) + (G)	(A) X (F)	J	EXP. MOD
	ARAP			167,123	1,267,560	237,124	1,671,807	(J) / (K)
	1.00		EXPECTED	(E)	(C) X (1-W) + (G)	(A) X (C)	K	0.65
	if applicable			485,076	1,267,560	830,381	2,583,016	

As the split point (primary) goes up each year, NCCI will count more of the claim in your calculation as primary. Consider with the .11 "w" value on a 50,000 claim.*

	Primary	Excess	Total
2012	5,000	45,000 x .11 = 4,950	9,950
2013	10,000	40,000 x .11 = 4,400	14,400
2014	13,500	36,500 x .11 = 4,015	17,515
2015	15,000	35,000 x .11 = 3,850	18,850
2016	?????	?????	?????

While it is too early to quantify the impact of the new split points, my feeling is if you have a lot of claims, the higher split point will probably increase your experience mod. Conversely, if you have very few claims, you should see a slight decrease in your mod.

---

* Please note this is an exhibit for illustration purposes only to show the impact of the increased split point. The numbers reflected in the total are not actually shown on the mod worksheet.

Section 3.4
Claims IQ

C✥MPOINTS

AN EFFECTIVE CLAIMS MANAGEMENT PROCESS REQUIRES EFFECTIVE COMMUNICATION.

Claims IQ is a process I developed to help disseminate claims information throughout an organization. Oftentimes a broker may communicate claims activity with senior management, but this information rarely makes it out of the corner office. You cannot create understanding, inspire commitment, and thus, impact performance unless you communicate this information where it's needed most—outside the walls of the corner office. Claims IQ helps you engage the people within your organization in order to achieve the results you want and improve the effectiveness of your claim management.

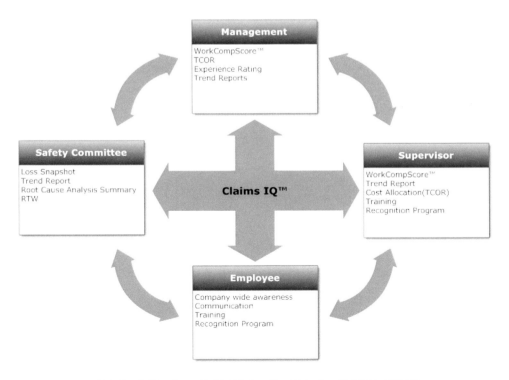

Adapted from the Balanced Scorecard by Robert S. Kaplan and Dave P. Norton. Harvard Business School Press, 1996
The Claims IQ™ Chart is copyrighted by Risk Management Inc. © 2014 All Rights Reserved.

Section 3.4.1

Management

Workers' Comp Scorecard

This is our high-level dashboard built for C-level positions. The process develops a target score and gives upper management a monthly performance score that can be drilled down for more granularity if needed. But you don't need a dashboard like the one found in my Compass RMS platform. Your broker can provide this information as part of your monthly or quarterly stewardship report. The important thing is, no matter how you get the information, be sure and make it a focal point of your manager/supervisor meetings. Management visibility to key cost drivers will impact accountability. What gets measured gets results!

Total Cost of Risk

As discussed earlier in the chapter, this is a calculation that should show how much product (or funding for a nonprofit) has to be generated to pay for claims. This is a great exercise to give tangible examples of how claims affect your organization.

Experience Rating – We also discussed experience rating earlier. Your broker probably has access to experience rating software that can produce a myriad of reports to help you better understand your experience mod. More importantly, these reports can give you keen insights into the cost of claims.

Trend Report

The Trend Report is similar to the mod trend report only it can trend a lot more than just claims data. For example, a trend report should always contain leading indicators like lag time and litigation rate.

Section 3.4.2

Supervisors

Workers' Comp Scorecard

This is primarily a management tool, but if supervisors know that management is paying attention to key indicators, such as lag time or safety audit exceptions, they will pay attention. Maybe I should have said what gets measured gets the supervisor's attention!

Trend Report

If there is a loss problem or a focus area for your safety program, it is critical that the supervisor understand the claims data to understand why you have created a targeted focus.

Cost Allocation

Some companies actually ding supervisor bonuses based on claim dollars spent. If the goal of the bonus program is to keep the supervisor engaged, this could have an opposite effect. Sometimes a bad claim happens despite good supervision. If the supervisor knows he may have lost his/her bonus, they may not care about future claims or quality of work for the rest of the bonus period. A better way to design a bonus program is to base it on trends. For example, use measurements such as the number of lost time claims, or the frequency of a particular nature of injury. Also, remember the TCOR calculation is a great way to help the supervisors understand the total cost of claims. If you can equate a claims dollar to a dollar of sales, you will have a strong tool to help create "top of mind awareness."

Let me give you an example. If you tell supervisors you had a $60,000 claim last month that may not resonate with them. If you tell them using the TCOR model it will resonate. Let's assume a company has a 5 percent profit margin. If you use the simple OSHA safety pays website we referred to earlier, you will see that your company has to produce $2,520,000 in sales to pay for the $60,000 claim. They understand how much product goes into $2.5 million of sales, thus creating the "top of mind awareness" you need from your supervisor.

Training

We have a whole chapter on training later in the book, but I'm referencing it now because it is an interdependent part of your organization's Claims IQ. Part of my Claims IQ process is to make sure supervisors understand your accident process, which includes reporting the claim, investigating the claim, and supporting the return to work (RTW) effort. The RTW training alone should be very detailed and based on both your organization's processes and the statutes in your state. I include RTW in my basic training for supervisors, but then drill down into much greater detail in a RTW specific training module, because supervisors are the number two reason RTW processes fail—number one being employee attitude. It is critical that supervisors have a clear understanding of your RTW process. The best opportunity to conduct this specific training is when they have an employee returning to work that will be under their supervision. You must use this opportunity wisely. This allows practical application of the training they have previously received. By monitoring their use of key training points when the RTW event actually happens, you can gauge their understanding of your process, thus putting knowledge into practice.

Loss

Recognition Program

Promoting safety is obviously your number one objective with a recognition program. But it should also be part of your organization's Claims IQ. Usually communication is negative and sounds something like this: "We are having too many claims" or "Joe's injury cost us all our bonus last month." You have to start by commending supervisors when their department does something well, such as having no accidents, and you need to make certain they communicate this "good news" to the employees they supervise. A culture based on positive reinforcement is necessary to build a strong Claims IQ.

C✦MPOINTS

> REMEMBER, DESPITE DOING EVERYTHING RIGHT, ACCIDENTS HAPPEN. HAVING THE SUPERVISORS ON BOARD WITH YOUR CLAIMS MANAGEMENT PROCESS WILL SIGNIFICANTLY REDUCE COSTS.

Section 3.4.3

Employee

C✦MPOINTS

> WHEN AN EMPLOYEE IS INJURED, THERE ARE A LOT OF EXTERNAL INFLUENCES THAT ARE TELLING THEM WHAT TO DO.

Companywide Awareness

Is there a companywide awareness of claims in your organization? If you are in an OSHA-regulated industry, the OSHA 300A is required to be posted on the employee bulletin board February 1 through April 30 each year. But you need to go beyond the OSHA log. Many organizations proudly display days without a lost time claim on banners outside their building, as well as throughout the facilities. I have seen others scroll accident information on TVs in their break rooms. Others may distribute information via payroll stuffers to keep the employees in the loop. Of course, as we discussed, the number one way to build employee awareness is through your supervisors.

Communication

COMPOINTS

> EMPLOYERS HAVE TO UNDERSTAND THAT THE INSURANCE COMPANY CANNOT BUILD TRUST WITH A CLAIMANT IF THE CLAIMANT DOESN'T FIRST TRUST THE EMPLOYER!

One of the biggest cost drivers in workers' compensation occurs when an employee retains counsel. Employers typically get offended when their employee sues them, but in many cases, the cause stems from the employee's lack of understanding of their rights and responsibilities. For a clearer understanding, consider that you are competing against a lot of external influence.

The injury occurs and now they're out of work. Hopefully, the employer files the claim and the adjuster places a phone call, which can typically be very impersonal, as part of their three-point contact (an adjuster should contact the employer/employee and medical provider within twenty-four to seventy-two hours of the claim). Oftentimes, the employer does not regularly communicate with the injured employee so the communication model looks like this:

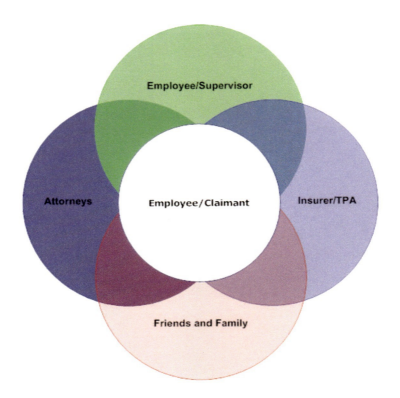

Consider that all these influences could be sending a mixed message to the employee. Whom the employee listens to for advice is usually dictated by the strength of the relationship. If the employee doesn't like their supervisor or trust the company, they will be more inclined to listen to other influences that might be advising them to seek legal advice. Also, and this is a powerful dynamic, you (the employer) may do everything right, but you quite possibly could be competing against the experiences that their friends and families may have had with other organizations, or maybe your employee has mistrust because of a previous experience with another employer. Your awareness of this dynamic is critical to your ability to successfully manage this process. The first line of defense is training to increase the employee's understanding of his or her rights and responsibilities, but this cannot be achieved by signing something at the time of hire. It has to be done continuously throughout the year. But you have to go even further—and this is not something you can outsource to your insurance carrier or TPA! You must show genuine care and concern for your employee when they have an injury and clearly outline their rights and responsibilities. Here is what the communication model should look like:

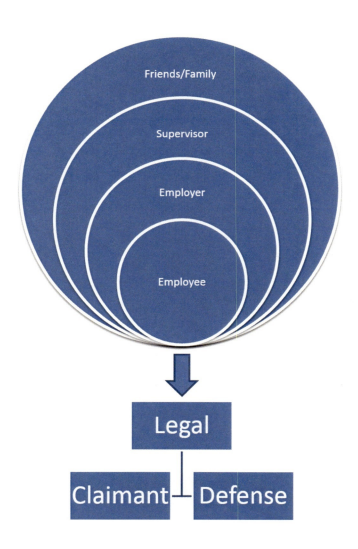

Notice, I have attorneys outside the center of influence model above. In my opinion, attorneys should not be a center of influence, but if you watch daytime television or look on the back of the phonebook you will see ads stating, "If you think you have been hurt," it is easy to see why employees, who feel vulnerable, reach out to the attorney for help. I want to be clear, having a good defense attorney is an important part of your claims management process. There are claims situations where the employee should get representation, but in my experience, this is a small percentage of claims. If you are like most employers, I am sure you would prefer not to have attorneys involved in the process. It's not only a huge cost driver, but it can also harm your organization's safety culture.

Here are some tips to improve your organization's Claims IQ and reduce litigation:

- Document, document, document! Have documentation that you explained the rights and responsibilities to the employee.
- After the injury, accompany the employee to the physician's office. The supervisor should not go into the treatment room unless the employee specifically requests their presence. An example of a situation where a supervisor could be present in a treatment room would be to assist with translation if the employee requested their assistance. Otherwise, the supervisor's presence could be viewed as an invasion of the employee's privacy.
- Send a "get well" card to the insured employee.
- Have the supervisor reach out to the employee on a regular basis (weekly) letting the employee know the employer is thinking about them.
- Initiate your RTW process quickly.
- If you can control direction to medical, choose a physician that you would go to if you were injured.

Training

We have discussed training already; however, I cannot stress enough the importance of proper, relevant, ongoing training. This is why my Claims IQ model lists training in all three areas—employer, supervisor, and employee. Take every opportunity that presents itself to improve understanding through communication and training.

Employee Recognition

If you only discipline and don't reward then the employees will not positively respond to any safety or claims program. We talked about setting up a near miss program. Proactive organizations use their near miss program to strengthen their safety culture. I believe proactive organizations also recognize employees who buy into their organization's Claims IQ. Here are some examples:

- Reward employees for reduction in lag time.
- Make a positive example of an employee who followed your RTW process.
- It is okay to recognize employees for days without a lost time claim, as long as there are no big incentives that could inhibit the reporting of claims.
- Recognize employees who contribute to your employee suggestion box with tips to improve safety and reduce future claims.

Section 3.4.4
Safety Committee

The role of the Safety Committee is to promote safety and help the organization reduce claims. From a claims perspective, the typical loss run does not provide much value to the Safety Committee. Here are some tips to help your Safety Committee understand your organization's Claims IQ.

Loss Snapshot

This is a summary of critical activities that have happened on a specific claim, including lag time to report the claim, the incurred amount of the claim, days away from work and/or days on restricted duty, and a summary of the next steps.

Loss Trend Report

This is more of a global report of all claims that should be broken down by location and department. Lag time should be included and addressed at every safety committee meeting.

Root Cause Analysis

Breaking down the root cause of claims is critical and you should do this on a claim, or multiple claims if time permits, during each meeting to use the process as a training opportunity. It will also trickle down to the supervisors that the root cause or accident investigation process is important!

Return to Work

It is critical to the Claims IQ of an organization that the Safety Committee discuss RTW at every safety meeting. If there aren't any specific lost time claims to discuss, then you should review the overall RTW process and look for opportunities to improve the process itself.

No doubt, experiencing Loss can be devastating on so many levels. As we move to the next letter in my PLOT process, we'll talk about how Organization can positively impact Loss. Quite often, one of the most costly mistakes a company can make is discounting the importance of a safety culture. In Organization, we are going to discuss safety culture, and as we do, I want to you keep this in mind—one of the biggest assets of a company is its safety culture! One of the biggest liabilities (Loss) of a company is the absence thereof!

---

[1] "Costs of Accidents," United States Department of Labor, website, https://www.osha.gov/SLTC/etools/safetyhealth/mod1_costs.html.

[2] *Employer Payment for Personal Protective Equipment*, Federal Register, Vol. 72 No. 220 (November 15, 2007), https://www.osha.gov/pls/oshaweb/owadisp.show_document?p_table=FEDERAL_REGISTER&p_id=20094.

[3] National Council on Compensation Insurance, "Experience Rating Update," pdf online (Fall 2011), 2, https://www.ncci.com/documents/exp_rating_update.pdf.

Chapter 4
Organization

> Leadership and employee engagement—an interdependent model for success.
>
> – National Safety Council

The National Safety Council noted that it has found four common elements in successful organizations: committed leadership and employee engagement, sound safety procedures, continuous risk reduction, and measuring and improving performance. Each year they have a tribute to "CEOs Who Get It." Take a minute and read the interviews (February 2014 issue, www.safetyandhealthmagazine.com). The common theme is the unwavering commitment from each leader to instill the four common elements noted above.

As I mentioned briefly before, I was recently at a workshop hosted by DuPont. DuPont has long been considered one of the thought leaders in safety, but the company didn't always think that way. DuPont began as a gunpowder manufacturer in 1802. When E. I. DuPont left France to escape the French Revolution in the early 1800s, his company relocated near Wilmington, Delaware. The industry in the early 1800s was anything but safe. Unfortunately, when a powder mill blew up it was usually a catastrophic event. E. I. DuPont earned a reputation for high quality and fairness, but also for workers' safety. Failure to follow safety standards was typically the root cause of the explosions, so to ensure that safety standards were met, he began constructing his managers' homes right beside the powder mills. You can imagine, with the manager's family next door, there was an increased focus on safety at the powder mills! Incidents went down almost immediately and the birth of modern safety was born. I am not suggesting anything this radical, but if safety is going to truly be first in an organization, there must be a "radical" understanding of its importance and the dire consequences if total engagement isn't present. "Sitting on a powder keg" takes on new meaning if safety isn't first in your organization.

Organization

Section 4.1
Safety Culture

The safety culture of an organization consists of the shared beliefs, practices, and mindsets that exist in an organization. The following factors will impact an organization's safety:

- Management, supervisor, and employee attitudes ("one bad attitude can pollute a hundred good attitudes")
- Management, supervisor, and employee assumptions and beliefs – Usually safety is a top-down effort and management assumes that employees will follow safety rules
- Management, supervisor, and employee values, myths, and stories
- Production and bottom line pressure – I do a lot of work in the manufacturing sector where there is an intense bottom line focus and safety is oftentimes a distant second
- Employee training and company motivation programs
- Employee involvement and buy-in

Section 4.1.1
Types of Safety Culture

It is important to remember safety is a journey not a destination. You cannot move from a zero safety culture to an interdependent safety culture overnight. It will take commitment, vigilance, and persistence. In the following chart, I correlate total cost of risk, lost workdays, and predatory culture directly to your safety culture. If you are an employer and you have registered your book (at www.managedcomp.net) you will gain access to a free, abbreviated version of my workers' comp scorecard.

Zero

A company with a **Zero Safety Culture** places little attention on safety. They have no safety staff because the company's focus is solely on production. Shortcuts are common, and very little regulatory knowledge exists in the organization. The company usually limits their safety efforts to the insurance carrier's annual drive-by. The goal is to get the carrier's risk control in and out as quickly as possible. This type of business is typically a start-up organization that is putting all their effort into production. If they stay in business, they will gradually move to the next level, the Limited Safety Culture.

Limited

A company with a **Limited Safety Culture** may have someone designated to handle safety. They are typically someone wearing many other hats who wants to spend as little time as possible on safety. Shortcuts are common, and very little regulatory knowledge exists in the organization. The company usually limits their safety efforts to the insurance carrier's annual drive-by, as well as some occasional training. Generally, a company at this maturity level begins to move towards the next level, Compliance, when one of the following occurs: an OSHA inspection, an insurance inspection, an injury (especially a serious one), an increase in the experience mod and/or the work comp rates, or a higher level manager brings information back to the organization that enlightens other managers on how little they know in the area of safety and health.

Compliance

When one of the aforementioned actions happens an organization typically moves into a **Compliance Safety Culture**. Typically, they will designate someone as the safety person and will try to set up policies and rules to enforce safety. This person is usually seen as a police-like figure because of their constant need to enforce safety rules and achieve compliance. Organizations that shift toward a Compliance Safety Culture may institute a safety incentive program and will usually implement a progressive discipline program. While this may generate some immediate results, the long-term results usually start to diminish as the person in charge of safety may shift their focus to other things. In many cases, safety incentive programs generally do not gain traction and usually are abandoned. Emphasis on compliance and safety incentives may impact positively motivated employees but rarely has an impact on neutral or negatively motivated employees.

Safety First

With a **Safety First Culture,** the organization devotes a lot of attention to promoting safety. Don't get me wrong, Safety First campaigns are run by some of the country's safest organizations. A company with a Safety First campaign goes beyond compliance. Safety is passed down to every level of the company. They post signs throughout the organization that tout things like "Days without a lost time claim." Communication is an important part of their safety culture. But many organizations stop here. They never ask the question, "If safety is first, what is second?" Second is having employees *feel* a part of the safety culture, and the importance placed on safety is as important as any other company objective. An organization with a Safety First Campaign will look for ways to improve training throughout the organization and improve their implementation of policies and procedures. They will shift their safety incentive program to a safety motivation program. They will also view the insurance carrier's risk control as a valuable part of their safety effort, and may even contract with a third party risk control to provide increased support to their safety efforts. Organizations with a Safety First culture will typically get favorable feedback from a safety perception survey. They also get favorable pricing from the insurance carriers!

Interdependent

When an organization has an **Interdependent Safety Culture** they are truly best in class. Less than 5 percent of the organizations in the United States have an Interdependent Safety Culture. These organizations have the lowest cost of risk because *everyone* in the organization is steadfast in making the organization a safe place to work. A company with an Interdependent Safety Culture has safety integrated in everything the organization does. The message is clear that safety is as important, if not more important, than production. An organization with an Interdependent Safety Culture broadens its Safety First mentality by including safety as part of its new hire orientation, ongoing training, annual performance reviews, and progressive discipline policies. An organization with an Interdependent Safety Culture also instills a culture where safety is pushed from the bottom up. This is done through the creation of a meaningful Safety Committee that is represented by all levels of the organization. Organizations with an Interdependent Safety Culture will almost always get favorable feedback from a safety perception survey and will quickly move to address any perceived deficiencies, which will further strengthen the safety culture of the organization. Finally, in an Interdependent Safety Culture there is an emphasis on wellness, and safety is stressed to the employees to make safety an extension of their mindset while they are away from work as well.

Section 4.2

Employee Perception Survey

I was at a recent conference and posed the question, "Perception is…?" Of course, everyone said reality. I injected a different perspective. Perception is expensive. There is often a wide gap between management's view of the organization's workplace safety program and the employee's perception, and this can be a huge cost driver. As I referenced above when detailing the successful strategies and steps that make up an Interdependent Safety Culture, a safety perception survey can be a valuable tool to help catapult you to a best in class safety culture. The perception survey is a tool designed to assess your employee's attitudes and beliefs about your workplace safety program. A great resource on this subject is the book *Yes You Can* by Dennis and Janie Ryan (www.compasshealthandsafety.com). It is designed to help you create your own safety perception surveys. Even if you outsource the safety perception survey, you may still wish to read this book to better understand the process. I have built my own safety perception survey tool inside Compass RMS, and I recommend two resources to outsource the perception survey. The standard-bearer on this subject is the National Safety Council. The upside to using the NSC Perception Survey is their experienced deployment team helps you manage the process. This will greatly reduce your timeline to implement the survey. You also receive some detailed benchmarking that can give your organization some great perspective. The NSC database is second to none. The downside to using NSC is the process can be expensive. Another issue of concern is that a survey like the NSC survey is not easily customized. The reason for this is due to the requirements for benchmarking. To have integrity to their database for benchmarking, the NSC has to have uniformity in their questions. If your organization wants a custom survey, and you wish to outsource, I would suggest contacting Dennis Ryan. He can provide you the consulting needed to develop a customized survey and can manage the database and the benchmarking reports for you.

Organization

In the introduction to his book, Dennis states,

> Before you can effectively plan for any health and safety improvements, you need to know the current status of your program. In other words, your program needs to be measured. Many companies have been prevented from plotting a true course to safety excellence due to limitations of the measurement approaches made available to them. There is currently no single health and safety measurement method that provides an accurate map of how companies can achieve world-class safety.[1]

He compares the value of **safety assessments** and **perception surveys** to what is commonly used today as an attempt to measure safety. Probably the most used methods are incident rates and loss runs from the insurance carrier. That is typically what an insurance carrier does when they underwrite and price your account. These certainly have some value, but oftentimes are not a true indicator or "measurement" of your workplace safety program. As I have said throughout this book, sometimes bad things just happen to organizations with good safety programs. Conversely, some organizations that have poor safety programs are just plain lucky, which may make them look good to the underwriter who doesn't look past the loss run.

Dennis goes on to say that achieving best in class safety is also dependent not only on the organization's safety "hardware," such as inspections, investigations, audits, and safety meetings, but also its "software," such as employee perceptions, attitudes, and values. Well said, Dennis!

Having touched upon safety assessments in the section on comP4, let's expand further on their role in a best in class safety culture. Dennis divides safety assessments into four categories:

- The **commencement stage**, or the birth of the program
- The **discovery stage**, when the company sets up the assessment process
- The **maturation stage**, when the assessment begins and the exceptions are being measured
- The **predicative stage**, when the assessment process begins to yield very little new information

Dennis contends that when the assessment process hits the predictive stage, it is time to make some changes. Enter the safety perception survey. This is the time when you want to put your finger on the pulse of your "software" and check the perceived value of your program. My feeling is an organization should consider conducting a safety perception survey every eighteen to twenty-four months, depending on employee turnover. As already stated, you can set up your own survey with the help of Dennis, or others that provide a similar service, or with the help of the National Safety Council. Here are the steps to get you started.

- **Develop a survey** – Decide on the survey questions. Dennis has some templates and so do some insurance carriers, or you can find a template on Zywave and BLR, which are subscription-based resources covered in more detail in the chapter on resources. Provide a "comments" section as this can help to gain insight into the employee's attitude. The comment section can be after each question or at the end of the survey. In an effort to standardize my perception survey, so I can benchmark results, I place the comments section at the end of the survey. This allows me to rapidly and inexpensively deploy the safety perception survey.

- **Test** – Test the survey for understanding. You must ensure that the respondents will understand the questions before rolling it out. If you use a time-tested perception survey, you can probably eliminate this step.

- **Sample** – Determine what percent of employees will participate in the survey. Certainly having everyone participate is a great way to make employees feel like they are part of the team, but the advantage of taking a smaller sampling is the cost savings. You will have employees out of work while completing the survey and you will have personnel administering and inputting the survey information, so a sampling reduces the amount of employees away from their positions.

- **Communicate** – Schedule a preemptive communication effort to announce the survey. This information needs to go out before the survey is launched so employees understand the purpose of the survey. The communication needs to stress the fact that the responses will be anonymous. This will help alleviate concerns about the survey.

- **Administer** – Determine how to administer the survey. My recommended method is to set up personnel in the break room, or wherever you hold employee meetings. Methods I've witnessed include a safety awareness month where they do activities throughout the month to promote safety awareness with the safety perception survey being one of the activities, and a safety breakfast where participants in the survey are treated to a biscuit and a drink. Ideas like this will certainly increase your participation and the "giveaway" (the safety incentive) will be positively received by the employees.

- **Analyze** – Analyze the data obtained from the survey. If you have high participation, you should yield a lot of data and should use a database to manage it effectively by converting the data into reports. You can use a simple database like Microsoft Access or use a third party to collect the data and provide you reports. There is a wealth of information you can glean from a safety perception survey, so it will be very important to have the reporting structure in place before the survey is launched. As you're deciding on the questions to ask in your survey, you can determine how you'd like the answers, once the surveys are completed, to translate into your reports.

Organization

- **Validate** – You must validate the information received in the survey. Once the information from the survey is available, you must validate the information to include employee comments. A good resource to vet this process is your Safety Committee, which we discussed earlier, is the Interdependent part of a best in class safety culture. The Safety Committee can investigate the validity of any concerns that might arise from the survey. You will want to differentiate between valid concerns and the complaints of a disgruntled employee. Having a large amount of surveys will give you trends. But you need to make sure if you have a small department, that you group them together as you want the respondents to remain anonymous.

- **Feedback** – Provide feedback of the results of the survey. It's important that if you seek employee comments to the survey questions, the employees will expect to see some action taken, or at a minimum, some communication about the survey results. If not, the credibility of the safety perception survey will be compromised.

- **Benchmarking** – You really need to decide what you are looking for. If you just want a simple analysis on your organization, you should consider building your own perception survey. If you want a little more advanced benchmarking on your organization and don't want to manage the development of the survey you should consider hiring a consultant that can help you construct a survey, such as Dennis. And if you want a turnkey solution that will give you benchmarking to compare your organization to other organizations, I would consider the National Safety Council. I personally developed a strategy somewhere in the middle.

- **Re-evaluate** – Re-evaluate survey results before conducting the next survey. You probably do not want to conduct a perception survey every year because of the time it takes to administer and act on the findings. When the time comes to administer your next survey, pull out your reports and action plans from the previous survey and review this information before you conduct your next survey. Your safety culture hopefully has changed, and the new data you seek may look much different.

If you are committed to improving your workplace safety program the addition of safety assessments and safety perception surveys are paramount to reaching your goal. A few more tips for your consideration. Management and supervisors need to take all feedback provided constructively. I have seen instances where feelings may get hurt. The purpose of this exercise is to improve safety! Management needs to remember that these processes not only allow you critical feedback from your employees, but will also help you develop training to improve your supervisor's performance. Your supervisors need your help. As I've stated and will state again, "Supervisors typically are not supervisors because they can supervise"!

Section 4.3

Safety IQ

COMPOINTS

ORGANIZATIONS WITH A HIGHER SAFETY IQ HAVE LOWER COSTS.

After studying hundreds of organizations over the years, I had an epiphany a few years ago. Organizations with higher Safety IQ (and Claims IQ) have lower work comp costs. So what is Safety IQ? I define Safety IQ as the entire organization's understanding and support of the workplace safety goals and objectives. A high Safety IQ is dependent on leadership. Dwight Eisenhower said, "Leadership is the art of getting someone else to do something you want done because he wants to do it." Think of the example I gave earlier about the leadership of E. I. DuPont. He certainly motivated his managers to *want* a safer workplace. Also, I started the chapter with the quote, "Leadership and employee engagement—an interdependent model for success." I would like to take the quote one step further and say, "To have safety engagement, you must make safety *awareness* part of the everyday culture." That is Safety IQ!

Here are some helpful tips to help you manage your Safety IQ:

- ☐ Do you know your organization's Safety IQ? The perception survey we just discussed is a great assessment tool.

- ☐ Do you have an action plan to manage your Safety IQ? This is something that must be done on a continuous basis. If employees sense that safety efforts ebb and flow, their attitude toward safety will also ebb and flow.

- ☐ Are your Safety Committee meetings meaningful? When is the last time senior management stepped into a management meeting? Consider Elane Stock, President of Kimberly-Clark Professional, and her National Safety Council interview. One of her personal goals is to "visit every plant around the globe each year and meet with local site leaders to understand each mill's safety performance and challenges, while also taking time to listen one-on-one to line workers."[2]

- ☐ When senior management participates, it demonstrates management commitment. I have a client with over 4,500 employees that is a Safety First organization. They place a great deal of emphasis on safety. They push safety 24/7. Each year they have a safety awards banquet for their drivers (they have a large fleet), and the president of the company takes time out of his busy schedule to present the awards each year. I have talked to several of the drivers, and they have commented on how much that means to them. One of the common themes of the industry's best safety cultures is senior management visibility.

- Do employees look after one another? Is team safety a part of your safety culture? Safety should be everyone's responsibility. Let's take a simple example. A grocery store employee is leaving for a lunch break and sees a puddle of liquid on the floor. Being aware of their environment, they safely navigate around the puddle and go onto lunch. If that same employee has a high Safety IQ, they will recognize that if the puddle is left unattended that another employee, or customer, could not be paying the same attention and have an accident. This simple illustration is the difference between individual safety and team safety.

- Does the organization's safety message stretch beyond the organization? Consider Craig Martin, President and CEO of Jacobs. Jacobs has a safety initiative called BeyondZero that goes beyond policies and procedures to promote a genuine culture of caring throughout their organization. As a recipient of SC 2014 CEOs That Get It, one of the accomplishments Martin outlined was a mandatory defensive driving course. What stuck out was that they offer the program to the employees' families. If employees don't practice safety at home, they probably do not come to work thinking safety.

- Does the company invest in leadership training? Your organization's safety efforts will be dependent on leadership and leadership is dependent on training. You have probably heard the expression "Some people are born leaders." Leaders aren't born! People are born with potential. Leaders are born through mentoring and training.

Section 4.3.1

Scoring Your Work Comp Program

COMPOINTS

HAVING AN OBJECTIVE SCORING SYSTEM FOR YOUR WORK COMP PROGRAM WILL RAISE ACCOUNTABILITY AND THAT ACCOUNTABILITY WILL IMPROVE RESULTS!

My company has developed a process to create a workers' comp scorecard, which I've made reference to already. Several brokers and consultants have their own work comp scoring process, so I would encourage you to ask your broker about how they help quantify your workplace safety program. If you don't have a resource available, you should check out www.reduceyourworkcomp.com. They have a very affordable process you can utilize if your broker does not have a process and an improvement plan that can help you raise your score. In their blog, they give the analogy that their work comp score works like a credit score. This is a good analogy. Think about your personal credit score. Your activities each month can favorably or negatively impact your credit score, and once a negative factor hits your score, it takes several years for this to come off your record. We have already talked about experience ratings, and it works kind of like a credit score. It tells insurers whether your claims experience is above average or below average, and when a claim stays on your mod for three years. But the experience rating mod is only one measure of a workplace safety program and is an annual calculation. Here are some attributes you will want to have in your scoring process:

- Your score should be updated at least every quarter (preferably every month) based on your stewardship plan.

- You should have a management dashboard. I see my credit score on my credit card statement every month. The score gives me a quick "snapshot" of the much more detailed information available to me if I need it. I know what range my credit score should be each month. If my credit score does not vary, I usually do not look very deep into the credit report. But if I do note a variance, I will drill down to find additional information that I need. My point is, for the report to have value to me, the score has to be easily visible and the ability to dig into the score for detailed information has to be easy. A dashboard can provide you this ease of management. Another benefit of the dashboard is that supervisors and employees quickly learn that management is watching! Talk about a sure fire way to ramp up Safety IQ.

- You should have a "what if" model for your scoring system so you can effectively focus your resources. Consider the same credit card report I get. When I drill down, they give me a simple "what if" tool so I can look at different scenarios and see how it will affect my score. This can be a very useful tool to help you prioritize and allocate your resources.

- You should be provided benchmarking data. On the personal credit score, you can easily see how you stack up in comparison to others. Why shouldn't you be able to do the same thing with your workplace safety program? A great free resource is located at www.bls.gov (search for injury and illness rates). Here you'll find a database where you can compare your **DART** (**D**ays **A**way, **R**estricted, and **T**ransferred) rate against other organizations with your SIC code. It even allows you to filter the results by the size of your company. This only looks at one aspect of your workplace safety program, but it is an effective (and free) benchmarking tool. I take the benchmarking process much further by comparing all of the aspects of our PLOT process for a more detailed evaluation.

Organization

Your score should be communicated to the insurance carrier. We will discuss this in more detail in the chapter on resources. The broker's ability to evidence stewardship to the insurance carrier will lower your insurance costs! Most brokers simply send loss runs to underwriters who price your account. It is important that they understand your commitment to safety and a scoring process shows them that you monitor this and have a continuous improvement process in place. They are used to seeing fancy stewardship plans from brokers (I would imagine you are too), but the insurance carriers rarely see the follow through. If your broker has a well-defined scoring process and has a history of follow through, you can get pricing on what your score *will be*, not what it is now!

YOU CANNOT PUT SAFETY FIRST IF SENIOR LEADERSHIP IS NOT ALL-IN!

The Safety IQ Process

- Management
    - Safety ROI (Return on Investment) – This does not need to done every year, but you should analyze your training methods and costs at least every three years to look for opportunities to increase your organizational efficiencies. This will also be a great opportunity to tweak your message.
    - Workers' Comp Scorecard – Have your broker work with you to develop an objective scoring method.
    - Safety Dashboard – Management has a lot of business objectives they have to track. Consider a dashboard report that summarizes your workplace safety program's leading indicators to keep management.
    - Lexample (leadership by example) – Find opportunities to get your senior leadership involved in safety.
    - Trickle Down Accountability – If you develop a trickle down accountability system, you will improve sustainability of your program.
- Supervisor
    - Training – This is one of the best investments you can make in your safety program.
    - Positive Reinforcement – Supervisors need to understand that employees are motivated by the carrot not the stick!

- Lexample – If supervisors don't walk the walk, your safety culture will suffer.
- Progressive Discipline – There are times when the carrot won't work. But supervisors have to be impartial when it comes to progressive discipline.

☐ Employee
- Understanding – If employees don't understand, they won't buy in.
- Training – If they don't understand, employees cannot comply with your safety rules.
- Buy in – If you don't engage your employees, it doesn't matter how good the training is. You won't reach them!
- Execution – No, this doesn't mean to bury injured employees in the back forty! This means that you have to train the employees then hold them accountable.

☐ Safety Committee (we discuss this at length in section on P3)
- Who should be on your safety committee?
- How often should you meet?
- How should you define your agenda?

---

[1] Dennis Ryan and Janie Ryan, *Yes You Can…Conduct your own safety perception survey* (Edmonton, Alberta: Compass Health and Safety Ltd., 2014), 11.

[2] Elane Stock, interview by National Safety Council, *Safety + Health* (February 1, 2014), http://www.safetyandhealthmagazine.com/articles/9758-CEOs-NSC?page=10.

Chapter 5
Training

> Sometimes one pays most for the things one gets for nothing.
>
> – Albert Einstein

The fourth part of the PLOT Process is Training. If you analyze best in class organizations, you will find one common denominator—a commitment to Training. Training is not an event, it is a continuous process. It is critical to remember employees learn differently! One method will not resonate with all of your employees.

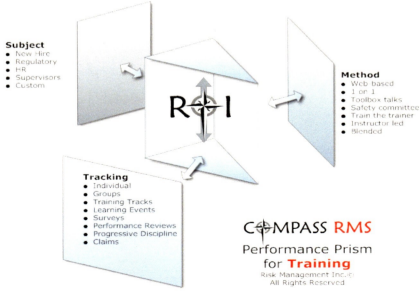

The Performance Prism is a performance measurement and management framework arising out of the work of the Centre for Business Performance at Cranfield University in the UK.

Training

The first step in Training is to commit to make it part of your company culture. The next step is to decide how to effectively deploy your training program. People learn in different ways, and one person's learning style isn't better than someone else. Some experts say there are as many as seven different learning styles, but most narrow it down to the three listed below:

- Auditory learners
- Visual learners
- Touch/experience learners

As an example of the different style of each of these groups, consider one of life's earliest lessons often taught to us by our mothers.

"Don't touch the hot stove, it will burn you!"

- Auditory learners heard their mother, believed the information, and never touched the stove.
- Visual learners watched their brother touch the stove, and never touched it.
- Experience learners touched the stove, but hopefully only once!

Most traditional safety training efforts are designed for auditory learners. If you develop training solely targeted at auditory learners, you will not engage a large percentage of your employees. This is why my new hire training method combines web-based training (auditory and visual learners) and a supervisor walkthrough (experience learners). Keep these three "learner" groups in mind as you design your training program. It is important to also consider different safety behaviors, which we have discussed earlier. Personality is a contributing factor to safety incidents, and different personality types learn differently. That is one of the reasons I introduced the Safety Quotient in the comP4 (P2) process.

I have divided Training into four categories: Subject, Method, Tracking, and ROI.

Section 5.1

Subject

To avoid overwhelming your organization, you must first decide on a strategic plan for your training. Your plan will be dictated by the industry you are in and your loss trends.

New Hire Training

The best opportunity to define your safety culture is during your new hire training. The challenge is *how* do you train them? Putting them in front of safety videos is the typical approach most companies take, but that has limited effectiveness. I was recently dining at a chain steakhouse. I could see a number of "new hires" huddled around a laptop that was playing safety training videos. I watched as they finished a module and then completed a paper quiz. Seemingly a really good process. As I passed by them on my way out, I asked how much they were learning. The feedback was not good, but it generally never is. The mind learns in different ways, and it is hard to sit in front of a monitor or TV screen for a couple hours watching safety training. Don't misunderstand, I believe in web-based training, but I think it needs a human element. I use a two-part process in my training. I have the new hire, or group of new hires, go through a new hire safety video covering the basics, and then I have the supervisor take them on a safety walkthrough with a checklist of activities. This method can reduce the training time by well over 50 percent, which is an impressive ROI, but we also get better traction with the development of the new hire. If you employ this method you will:

- ☐ Improve the employee's Safety IQ
- ☐ Reduce the training time
- ☐ Develop a relationship between the supervisor and the employee
- ☐ Improve the Safety IQ of your supervisors

Regulatory

If you are in an OSHA-regulated industry, you have required training. Here are some of the required training programs. There also could be required training for things like sexual harassment (for example, CA AB1825 in California) or DOT training.

Accident and Illness Recording and Reporting	Laser Safety
Anhydrous Ammonia Storage & Handling	Liquefied Petroleum Gas (LPG) Safety Plan
Blood-Borne Pathogens Safety	Lockout/Tagout (Control of Hazardous Energy)
Compressed Gases (General)	Machine Safeguarding
Confined Space Entry (Permit-Required)	**Material Handling & Crane Safety**
Dipping & Coating Operations	Means of Egress
Electrical Safety Plan	Medical and Exposure Record Access

Training

Emergency Action Plan*	**Mechanical Power Presses**
Ergonomics Plan	**Personal Protective Equipment**
Fire Extinguishers (Portable for Employee Use)	**Power Transmission/Generation**
Fire Prevention Plan*	**Powered Industrial Truck**
First Aid Program	Powered Platforms for Building Maintenance
Flammable & Combustible Liquids Safety	**Process Safety Management**
General Working Spaces – Housekeeping	**Radiation (Ionizing) Safety**
Grain Handling Facilities	**Recordkeeping Practices & Reporting**
Hand Tool Safety	**Respiratory Protection**
Hazard Communication Program	Safety & Health Management Policy
Hazardous Waste Operations & Emergency Response (General)	Safety Committee Organizational Plan
	Safety Signs & Safety Colors
Hearing Conservation	Spray Finishing
Hot Work (Cutting/Welding)	Telecommunications
Indoor Air Quality	Ventilation
Laboratory Safety	Walking-Working Surfaces
Ladder Safety	

Programs listed in **bold** indicate a mandatory written program is required

If required by a specific OSHA standard. Employers with fewer than ten employees may communicate these plans orally instead of in writing.

In addition to the required regulatory training, OHSA recommends the following training:

- ☐ Safety Rules for Employees
- ☐ Disaster Recovery Plans
- ☐ Safety Committee or Safety Teams
- ☐ Safety Rules for Contractors
- ☐ Workplace Violence Prevention Plan

- Return to Work Program
- Medical Management Program
- Job Safety Analysis Program Ergonomic Evaluation Process
- New Employee Orientation Program

Human Relations

More and more companies are going to HRIS systems, which allow employees to self-select their benefits. Having training modules on topics like Cobra and FMLA allow the HR department to push out reliable information to employees enabling them to better understand the complex laws. This can save a lot of time for your HR staff, which allows them to invest more time into training and compliance. HR departments are also turning to web-based content to train managers on topics like performance reviews and progressive discipline. Another growing area of training is Wellness Training. A meaningful wellness program is a proven strategy to reduce your workers' compensation costs.

Supervisor Training

We previously discussed supervisor training, but I wanted to drill a little deeper into this subject. One of the characteristics of a company with an Interdependent Safety Culture is the time those organizations spend teaching supervisors how to lead.

In addition to leadership training, the supervisors also need OSHA training. The National Safety Council has an excellent resource called the Supervisors Safety Development Program. I am developing a series for my clients where I will teach the course over an eleven-month period. It is a sixteen-part program that includes the following topics: safety management, communication, safety and health training, employee involvement, safety and health inspections, incident investigation, industrial hygiene, personal protective equipment, ergonomics, hazard communication, regulatory issues, machine safeguarding, hand and portable power tools, material handling and storage, electrical safety, and fire safety. I am also working on a training program to help supervisors understand and manage different behavior types.

Custom Training

Don't reinvent the wheel. If you are conducting safety training, chances are you can get a free resource from your broker or your insurance carrier. For example, if you get a training outline on lockout/tagout, you can easily give your training a customized look by placing pictures of your facility over the stock images. Most brokers have access to excellent risk management resource libraries, but the training and resources will be stock training. Spend a couple extra minutes customizing the training or handouts to engage your employees. Employee engagement is the key to improving your safety culture.

Training

Section 5.2
Method

Web-based Training

Many organizations are turning to web-based training. You can create web-based training without an LMS (Learning Management System), but you will not be able to track the results. The LMS enables you to assign and track training. If you do purchase an LMS, you will need to purchase training from a third party or create your own training. Most of my clients do both. They utilize my library for the compliance and customized risk management training I have created—for example I have a CWCC program (Certified Workers' Compensation Coordinator)—and I give them an authoring tool to create their own company specific presentations, including customer service, product information for their customers, and marketing materials. I have seen a lot of creativity, and web-based authoring tools are getting easier to use and more affordable. More on this topic in my section on Resources.

From a training perspective, web-based training offers many benefits:

- ☐ It is easily accessible
- ☐ Costs are going down
- ☐ It allows rapid development
- ☐ It is easy to customize
- ☐ It allows self-paced learning
- ☐ It can give participants instant feedback
- ☐ It is easy to update training
- ☐ You can buy training to meet your organization's specific needs
- ☐ If you are using an LMS, the results can be tracked

One-on-One

Nothing beats one-on-one training. This works best during new hire training so you can connect the employee to the safety culture of your organization. One-on-one training is also a good method for progressive discipline training (coaching).

Toolbox Talks

This method was developed for contractors to do training at the jobsite (hence the name), but it is also the name associated with small ten- to twenty-minute training sessions generally led by the supervisor. BLR and Zywave both have a large number of toolbox talks available for your use, and a great free resource is www.safetytoolboxtalks.com.

Safety Committee

The Safety Committee is a good place to conduct training. Many organizations use this as an opportunity to train the trainer as well.

Train the Trainer

Whether it is the Safety Committee or the supervisors, one of the most effective ways to conduct training throughout an organization is the train the trainer method. You train a group of people and they in turn go out and train the rest of the employees. This can be a very effective method if you have multiple locations. Below are some solutions to concerns that may be encountered when using this method of training.

- **I don't have any resource information.**

    Most brokers have a resource (like Zywave) that provides you a "train the trainer kit" that includes a trainer outline, handouts, sign-in sheet, and a quiz.

- **I don't have the resources to train the trainers.**

    Consider having your broker and your carrier come in and lead the training. Another creative approach is to show the web-based training module to the trainers and give them an instructor-led training program from a compliance expert like BLR.

- **I have multiple locations.**

    A cost-effective tool to push out training, as well as other company information, is through online meeting software. I use GoToMeeting as my online meeting vendor. It is affordable and easy to use. Most of the "train the trainer" kits contain a PowerPoint presentation, which works great with GoToMeeting.

- **I have a large percent of Hispanic employees.**

    Most of the train the trainer materials from vendors are bilingual, so you can get this information from your broker in English, Spanish, or both.

Instructor-led

If you are fortunate enough to have an in-house trainer, you can still re-purpose the train the trainer material. One of the huge advantages of having a company trainer is the consistent, well-designed message. One of the downsides is you lose the opportunity to empower supervisors to lead your safety effort. Also, if your trainer leaves you may have a void in your training program.

Blended

One of most effective ways to engage your learners is by taking a blended approach of all of the training methods listed above. For example, you may utilize web-based training for new hires, but utilize toolbox talks for ongoing training. Technology is advancing at a rapid pace and you will continue to see huge advances to the blended learning approach. We began the section on Training by discussing that employees learn differently; therefore, an effective and meaningful training program recognizes this fact and utilizes a blended approach as the preferred method.

Section 5.3

Tracking

In today's regulatory and litigious environment, documentation is more important than ever! In addition to OSHA, many of your customers may ask to see your training records. While this has been the case for contractors, for many years I am seeing it trickle down into other industries. For example, I do a lot of work with food processors. Their customers are now looking at safety as part of their plant audit process. Also, consider nonprofits in this discussion. Accrediting organizations are now including safety in the audit process. I believe the reason is simple: organizations with accountable and effective safety programs have higher quality standards. One of the easiest ways to audit safety is to review the training records. You don't need an LMS to track training, but you will need some kind of a database, such as Microsoft Access. If tracking is important to you, I would strongly recommend a LMS.

If you do have an LMS, you can track your training in the following methods:

- **Individual Tracking**

    This is best used for the new hire orientation process when you onboard a new employee.

- **Group Tracking**

    This is helpful if you assign training by department. Another great feature of group tracking is you can give your supervisors control over the training of employees that report to them.

Pushing the ability to assign and track training to your supervisors is a standard feature in most Learning Management Systems.

- **Training Tracks**

If you use group tracking and someone is put in a group, they are assigned training. But it is a one and done process. Whatever is assigned to them is assigned to all of those in the group at one time. This may overwhelm learners. Consider putting employee's on a training track, which simply means training is assigned over a period of time rather than all at once.

- **Learning Events**

This is a fancy name for toolbox talks. When you push out training to your entire organization at one time this is called a Learning Event. For example, a food processor with 800 employees has twelve departments, two locations, and two shifts. That means at a minimum forty-eight toolbox talks have to take place. That is a lot to keep up with, so you will want to make sure you have a database to track this. If OSHA comes in, they will want to see your training records.

- **Surveys**

Most LMS platforms have a survey tool. I have already talked about the safety perception survey, but you might also want to use your LMS to track things like a voluntary wellness survey or some other internal survey that your company pushes out to employees. I actually use the survey module to assign training. For example, my wellness survey gives the employee the opportunity to request training based on a specific survey response.

- **Performance Review**

Many LMS cross over to the HRIS (Human Resource Information System) space and include talent management pieces such as employee performance reviews. The ability to track reviews and compare data with your workers' compensation claims was previously discussed.

- **Claims**

Being able to track training can have huge implications on your workers' comp claims. For example, if an employee is not following safety you may be able to assert a willful misconduct defense. One of the prerequisites for a willful misconduct defense is systematic training records. Since supervisors are such a pivotal part of the RTW process, you should review when the last time a supervisor went through your RTW training to ensure they understand your RTW process.

Training

Section 5.4

Return on Investment (ROI)

Most safety vendors try to come up with a ROI model to sell their safety platform or services to upper management. Getting buy-in from management is challenging because quantifying the ROI is so difficult. OSHA has long stated that every dollar invested in safety yields a return of four to six dollars. That is a pretty compelling ROI, but sometimes it is not enough to grab management's attention. We have talked about TCOR in a previous chapter being an effective tool to measure direct and indirect costs. However, focusing exclusively on the direct and indirect costs associated with accidents does a disservice to well-run safety organizations. Engaging leadership, the ability to diagnose issues and act preventatively to correct them, and the supportive and collaborative nature of an Interdependent Safety Culture spill over into broader organizational effectiveness. Dividends include better quality, greater productivity, improved risk profile, higher employee morale, and lower turnover, but all these are soft reasons to invest in training. BLR has a simple formula to help you measure ROI:

$$\text{ROI}(\%) = ((\text{monetary benefits} - \text{training costs}) \div \text{training costs}) \times 100.$$

EXAMPLE

Assume that as a result of a new safety training program, an organization's accident rate declines 10%, yielding a total annual savings of $200,000 in terms of lost workdays, material and equipment damage, and workers' compensation costs. If the training program costs $50,000 to implement, the ROI would be 300%.

ROI = ((200,000 − 50,000) ÷ 50,000) x 100 = 300%

In this example, for every dollar spent on training, the organization gained a net benefit of three dollars.

To get the figures for ROI analysis, you will need historical TCOR information (benchmark your current TCOR calculation versus last year's TCOR calculation); keep track of training costs, including the cost of design and development, promotion and administration, delivery (staff or technology), and materials and training facilities; Learning Management System; trainee wages; and training evaluation. After training, keep track of monetary benefits, including labor savings, reduction in lost workdays and workers' compensation costs, productivity increases, and lower turnover costs.

If you are just starting this process, here is a simple way to get started:

- Develop a TCOR calculation for next year's safety training ROI calculation.
- Analyze your current training program to look for operational efficiency. I understand that for some organizations implementing a best in class training program will increase costs in the short term, but there are still opportunities for organizational efficiency. Consider a recent client I just onboarded. They are in a high turnover industry and send out about 4,000 W-2s a year for a workforce of 1,400. This industry is on OSHA's targeted list. With their high turnover, the new hire safety orientation has increased importance. With our two-prong approach for new hire training, we were able to reduce the new hire orientation from 132 minutes to 37. This saved the organization $47,500 and improved the employee's Safety IQ. How? Because we invested the resources up front to create a customized program.

In short, results-oriented training is crucial to improving your organization's safety culture. Be sure you evaluate the business need and match the training to that need by a thorough process of discovery, design, development, implementation, and execution for results. Always remember that training is not an event, it's a process. If you follow this course, you will maximize the return on your investment! And remember, your biggest investment is your people.

Chapter 6
Return to Work: Use of Light Duty Work

AN OVERVIEW OF RETURN TO WORK PROGRAMS THROUGHOUT THE UNITED STATES

This section was contributed by Greg Presmanes, Partner with Bovis, Kyle, Burch, and Medlin in Atlanta, Georgia.

Section 6.1
Introduction

Along with the downfall of the US economy and the staggering unemployment rate, the business world is suffering further from lost work days due to employee sickness or injury.[1] The National Safety Council "estimates there are over 80,000,000 lost work days due to occupational injuries or illness."[2] Furthermore, the Bureau of Labor and Statistics reports, "1.2 million employees lost an average of seven days due to their injury or illness."[3] The annual costs associated with employee injury or illness, including medical care and the decrease in productivity, comes to $1.25 trillion.[4] The question becomes: what can employers do to reduce the amount of time employees remain out of work?

The American Academy of Orthopaedic Surgeons has long evaluated this problem and strongly suggests that the best outcome, both for employers and for injured workers, is to return employees to the work force as soon as possible.[5] Those who remain out of work for extended periods of time often never return to work.[6] They suffer from increased pain and depression, and as a result take longer to heal and require more medical intervention than other patients.[7] J. Mark Melhorn, with the University of Kansas School of Medicine, posits that "[o]ne of the roadblocks to getting people back as productive members of the work force is the very thing set up to protect them, the workers' compensation systems run by the various states and the federal government."[8] Margaret Spence, a board certified Workers' Compensation consultant, is similarly concerned that the workers' compensation system as a whole is partially to blame.[9] She notes that it is "riddled with loopholes, litigation, layers of rules and regulations and it does not provide employers with adequate guidelines or resources to understand the importance of implementing return to work policies."[10] In fact, she opines that many employers receive no information on designing effective Return to Work programs until an adjuster is managing their claim file.[11]

The express purpose often enumerated in state statutory provisions governing workers' compensation is to compensate injured workers during their recovery and return them to suitable employment at the earliest possible time. Indeed, it is "the prime aim of a compensation system . . . to help workers recover from work-related accidents and return to the workplace."[12] It is surprising then, that employers often fail to take a proactive role in returning their employees to work. Many times employers feel they can offer no meaningful jobs within the employee's work restrictions.[13] In the alternative, employers worry that injured workers who do not want to be at work will display attitude problems, which will in turn lead to decreased productivity and morale amongst other employees.[14] By the same token, employees may be reluctant to return to their former jobs following an injury because they feel a lack of support from their employer.

In an effort to combat these issues, states have enacted legislation to provide a smooth transition between the work-related injury and returning to the workplace. The purpose of this chapter is to explore state statutory codes governing return to work programs and highlight those states that have implemented effective procedures. Section 6.2 outlines specific features found in state statutes that provide both legal and financial incentives to return to work. While the list is not exhaustive, these include the light duty job offer and employee benefit termination, premium discounts or dividends, medical and vocational rehabilitation services, special funds, requirements that employers reinstate injured workers, required job searches, and preferred worker programs. The law must often intervene to govern the return to work process, but perhaps states should reevaluate existing law and modify it to more effectively address return to work. Section 6.3 provides suggestions for state legislators with regard to identifying important considerations in returning injured employees to work and implementing successful return to work programs.

Section 6.2
State Statutory Code

As stated above, states have attempted to address the needs of employers and injured employees with regard to fashioning return to work programs, with varying results. In many instances, the employee voluntarily returns to work when he recovers from his job injury. These results are often attributable to the policies of specific employers and not related to statutory incentives. However, when litigation ensues, the law must step in and facilitate the return to work process.

Section 6.2.1

Financial Incentives

One of the biggest concerns for employers and employees alike following a work injury is financial loss. Therefore, a majority of states provide for some financial incentive to return injured workers to the workplace. As discussed more fully below, many states offer negative financial incentives to employees to return to work by cutting off temporary disability benefits if the employee refuses a suitable job offer. On the other hand, some states provide a money back reward to employers who return former employees to work at their pre-injury wages. Both of these practices demonstrate an attempt by state legislators to entice employers and employees to actively participate in the return to work process by appealing to their pocketbooks.

The Light Duty Job Offer: Employee Benefit Termination

A light duty job offer in the context of workers' compensation claims can be an effective tool to return injured employees to work in that it can both reduce the exposure and length of the claim. A majority of states allow employers to suspend or terminate disability benefits when an employee refuses an offer of suitable employment.[15] As such, this is likely the most widespread and direct incentive to return injured employees to work. Georgia is paradigmatic of this type of incentive. The pertinent portion of GA. CODE ANN. §34-9-240 (2008) reads:

> If an injured employee refuses employment procured for him or her and suitable to his or her capacity, such employee shall not be entitled to any compensation ... at any time during the continuance of such refusal unless in the opinion of the board such refusal was justified.[16]

States differ in defining what constitutes "suitable" employment, and what acts comprise refusal of said employment such that employers can lawfully suspend or terminate disability benefits. Furthermore, while many states allow employers to terminate or suspend benefits during the period of refusal of suitable employment, if a judge or workers' compensation board finds the refusal justified, the employer may not terminate benefits for such refusal. Lastly, in most states the period of forfeiture of benefits lasts only during the duration of refusal. Thus, if a claimant initially refuses the job offer, but later changes his mind and accepts the proffered job, the suspension of benefits ceases.[17]

"Suitable" Employment

By way of example, a Georgia employer may offer an injured worker an available light duty job pursuant to a Form WC-240(a)[18] in which the employer provides the job analysis or the "essential job duties to be performed, including hours to be worked, the rate of payment, and a description of the essential tasks to be performed."[19] The employer must submit said job offer to the authorized treating physician for approval with a simultaneous copy to the injured worker's attorney. Once the job is approved by the authorized treating physician, it must then be offered to the employee.

The Supreme Court of Georgia has defined "suitable" employment as that which is commensurate with the employee's "capacity or ability to perform the work within his physical limitations or restrictions."[20] In a well-established decision, the Georgia Court of Appeals held that an illegal worker was not entitled to benefits because his employer had offered him "suitable" employment as a delivery truck driver.[21] The employee could perform the job physically, but because he was an illegal alien, he was unable to obtain a valid driver's license.[22] The fact that the employee could not accept the job because he could not produce a valid driver's license was of no consequence, as the term "suitable to his capacity refers only to the employee's capacity or ability to perform the work within his physical limitations or restrictions, and not whether he has, or does not have, legal residency or a driver's license."[23]

Justifiable Refusal of Light Duty Job Offer

Most courts require some conscious act on the part of the employee in refusing suitable employment before allowing the employer/insurer to suspend disability benefits. In Georgia, if an employee fails to report to work at the appointed date and time, or in the alternative, if the employee arrives at work but declines to begin work and claims he is physically incapacitated, such employee has effectively "refused" the proffered job such that an employer would be entitled to unilaterally suspend disability benefits.[24]

Once it has been determined that the light duty job is "suitable" to the employee's capacity, a determination must be made as to whether the employee's refusal of said offer is justified. While the judge or board usually has wide discretion in this area, the Supreme Court of Georgia has found that in order for an employee's refusal of a job offer to be justified, that refusal "must relate to the physical capacity of the employee to perform the job; the employee's ability or skill to perform the job; or factors such as geographic relocation or travel conditions which would disrupt the employee's life."[25] The employee is not justified, however, in refusing work due to personal reasons unrelated to work.[26]

For example, Georgia courts have held that injured employees are justified in refusing suitable employment when they lack the skills to perform the job. In *City of Adel v. Wise*, the Georgia Court of Appeals found it was not unreasonable for a nurse to refuse a typing job that she was physically capable of performing, but lacking in skills.[27] Likewise, an employee is justified in refusing employment that would disrupt his life. In *Clark v. Georgia Kraft Co.*, the court held an employee was justified in refusing suitable work that required him to work in an area of the plant that was not air-conditioned because the lack of air could adversely affect the employee's prosthetic arm and ability to work.[28] Additionally, it is reasonable for an employee to refuse work that requires him to relocate his home because it is disruptive.[29] On the other hand, Georgia courts have not permitted employees to refuse work due to inconvenient hours.[30]

State Trial Return to Work Programs

Although employers in some states can unilaterally suspend benefits when employees unjustifiably refuse offers of suitable employment, states like Georgia and North Carolina have enacted trial return to work programs that appear to counteract or negate the employer's ability to suspend employee benefits. In North Carolina, an employee may attempt a trial return to work for a period not to exceed nine months.[31] During this period of time, the employee shall collect compensation, which may be owed for partial disability.[32] If the trial return to work is unsuccessful, the employee may continue to collect total disability compensation.[33] Similarly, in Georgia, if an employee attempts the proffered job, but is unable to perform for more than fifteen working days, the employer must immediately reinstate weekly disability benefits.[34]

Temporary Alternative Work Opportunities

Similarly, some states, like New Hampshire and Rhode Island, require that employers develop temporary alternative work opportunities for injured employees.[35] The New Hampshire Department of Labor outlines the procedure by which employers make such work available to an injured employee.[36] Employers can execute a task analysis form whereby they provide the daily tasks performed by the employee prior to his injury.[37] This form is then presented to the employee's physician and can assist him in determining what physical restrictions the employee may have as a result of the injury.[38] By the same token, the task analysis form can help the employer develop an appropriate alternative duty plan to bring the injured employee back to work quickly.[39]

Some employers have specific alternative duty positions set aside in advance for this purpose, and therefore the task analysis form can be forwarded quickly to the treating doctor for approval.[40] However, if the injured employee refuses such temporary alternative work, the employer may petition the Department of Labor to reduce or terminate the employee's compensation.[41]

Premium Discounts or Dividends

By contrast, no states statutorily mandates that insurance companies offer premium discounts or dividends when employers reinstate employees following work injuries, but Colorado and California are two such states that provide for premium rebates when an injured worker is returned to work under certain circumstances. By way of example, Colorado provides that the commissioner of insurance shall include a "premium dividend of up to ten percent if an employer reemploys injured employees at their pre-injury wages including any wage increases to which such employees would have been entitled had the employee not been injured."[42]

Premium dividends are a tangible reward for those employers who have reduced their workers' compensation losses below original expectations for a given policy period. It logically follows that when employers reinstate injured employees they are significantly decreasing their costs, as the worker has returned to suitable employment and is contributing to productivity rather than adversely affecting the bottom line. As such, this money back approach provides the employer with a positive financial incentive to return injured workers to employment at their pre-injury wages.

Section 6.2.2
Rehabilitation[43]

The purpose of rehabilitation assistance is to "restore an injured worker's earnings capacity as nearly as possible to that level that the worker was earning at the time of injury and to return the injured worker to suitable gainful employment in the active labor force as quickly as possible in a cost-effective manner."[44] By enacting statutes that assist injured workers in acquiring gainful employment, state legislators have recognized that physical recovery is not the only obstacle in returning to work. In fact, rehabilitation can be one of the most effective devices to return injured employees to work. A Michigan study conducted by the vocational rehabilitation division found that about 60 percent of the workers referred to vocational rehabilitation in the first ninety days of disability returned to work, whereas only about 29 percent of the workers referred after two years returned to work.[45] These numbers suggest that providing rehabilitation services is crucial to dispelling the tendency of injured employees to view workers' compensation as an "extended vacation plan."[46]

A majority of the states have some statutory provision for rehabilitation services for injured employees in order to encourage early return to work.[47] Most of these programs mandate employers or their insurance carriers fund rehabilitation services to assist employees with living expenses and vocational training.[48] Employers are enticed to participate in rehabilitation because they hope the employee is successful in the program and can return to the work force, thereby significantly decreasing or even terminating the disability payments for which the employer may be liable.[49] Conversely, employees have an incentive to participate because some states, like New Hampshire, suspend or terminate disability payments if the employee is uncooperative or refuses to accept vocational rehabilitation.[50]

Generally, there are two types of rehabilitation services that arise in the workers' compensation context. First, all states require that employers provide medical rehabilitation services related to the employee's job injury.[51] The goal of medical rehabilitation is to repair the injured employee physically in order to return him to the work force as quickly as possible.[52] Medical rehabilitation generally consists of "exercise and muscle conditioning, under the supervision of a physician, to restore a person to maximum usefulness" or any other treatment or therapy recommended by the injured employee's physician.[53] Many times an injured employee can return to work following medical rehabilitation alone.

On the other hand, vocational rehabilitation focuses on the ability of the injured worker to return to work and is typically offered to those employees who have incurred significant limitations as a result of the job injury, have few transferable skills, and cannot return to work with their former employer.[54] These services can often include many of the following: counseling and guidance with job placement, job seeking skills, job accommodations, skills training, college training, physical and emotional restorative services, driver training, and vehicle and home modification.[55] Typically, the goal is to return the injured employee to work with his former employer, or in the alternative, to return the employee to similar work with another employer, different work with another employer, or finally, to provide training to the employee so that he might obtain employment in another occupational field.[56]

A number of states, including Hawaii and Kansas, have enacted comprehensive vocational rehabilitation schemes that are not mandatory for the injured employee.[57] Hawaii provides that an injured employee may enroll in a rehabilitation plan, and the employee and certified provider of rehabilitation services shall submit an initial report to the employer detailing an assessment of the employee's current medical status, disability, physical or psychological limitations, and a job analysis, among others.[58] More importantly, an injured employee may continue to collect temporary total disability benefits while enrolled in a rehabilitation plan or program if the employee is not earning wages during the period of enrollment.[59] If he does earn wages for work he performs under the program, he shall be entitled to the difference between his average weekly wage at the time of his injury and the wages received under the program.[60]

By contrast, other jurisdictions require that the employer provide rehabilitation services to an injured employee, recognizing that the primary purpose behind workers' compensation is to restore the injured employee to gainful employment.[61] Kentucky provides: "[w]hen as a result of the injury [an injured employee] is unable to perform work for which he has previous training or experience, he shall be entitled to such vocational rehabilitation services, including retraining and job placement, as may be reasonably necessary to restore him to suitable employment."[62] Louisiana, Maine, Michigan, Minnesota, New Hampshire, Oklahoma, and Oregon, among others, also entitle injured workers to vocational rehabilitation services and have statutes similar to Kentucky.

Finally, in a few states, such as Iowa, an injured employee is entitled to a $100 weekly payment from the employer, in addition to other benefits, during each week he is actively participating in a vocational rehabilitation program.[63] However, these payments are generally made for a period not to exceed thirteen weeks, unless the circumstances suggest that a continuation of services will accomplish rehabilitation of the injured employee.[64]

Section 6.2.3

Special Funds: The Second Injury Fund

States have recognized that employers may be reluctant to hire employees with preexisting permanent disabilities, and therefore nearly all jurisdictions[65] have developed or have had second injury funds that are generally formed to "encourage employers to hire disabled workers by limiting, in the case of further injury, their liability for compensation payments to amounts only applicable to the latest injury."[66] Second injury funds reimburse employers who hire disabled workers for workers' compensation benefits if that worker suffers a second or subsequent injury.[67] In other words, if an employee is hired with a permanent preexisting condition and later suffers a subsequent injury that exacerbates his previous disability, the employer is typically only responsible for the portion of the disability caused by the subsequent injury.[68] In this way, second injury funds operate as "apportionment devices" such that the cost of a workers' compensation claim is distributed "from an individual employer to the entire workers' compensation system, as funded by all employers."[69]

Second injury funds originally functioned as indirect return to work programs, in that they "promote[d] [the] social policy of encouraging employers to hire or retain such employees" with permanent preexisting disabilities.[70] However, in recent years, many states have come to view such funds as "expensive and counterproductive."[71] With the passage of the Americans With Disabilities Act in 1992 and specific state laws prohibiting discrimination of the disabled in hiring decisions, state legislators began to reexamine the purpose of their Second Injury Funds.[72] By 2005, many states, including Alabama, Colorado, Connecticut, Florida, Kansas, Kentucky, Minnesota, Maine, Nebraska, New Mexico, Oklahoma, Utah, and South Dakota, as well as the District of Columbia, had limited or eliminated their Second Injury funds.[73] Georgia followed in 2006.[74]

Section 6.2.4

Injured Worker Reinstatement

Some states require that employers reinstate injured employees if there is work available to which the employee could be assigned. The policy still places an emphasis on returning the injured worker to work, but these provisions place the burden on the employer to make room for injured employees or face monetary penalties. In Arkansas:

[a]ny employer who without reasonable cause refuses to return an employee who is injured in the course of employment to work, where suitable employment is available within the employee's physical and mental limitations, upon order of the Workers' Compensation Commission, and in addition to other benefits, shall be liable to pay to the employee the difference between benefits received and the average weekly wages lost during the period of the refusal, for a period not exceeding one (1) year.[75]

Like Arkansas, these states usually impose time limits on the period to which this applies. In Maine, the employer's obligation to reinstate the employee generally expires after one year from the date of injury, but can continue for three years if the employer has over 200 employees.[76]

Moreover, most states take into account various factors in determining whether an employer must reinstate an injured worker. In Maine, in order to facilitate the placement of an injured employee, an employer must make "reasonable accommodations for the physical condition of the employee unless the employer can demonstrate that no reasonable accommodation exists or that the accommodation would impose an undue hardship on the employer."[77] Maine courts consider the size of the employer's business, the number of employees employed, the nature of the employer's operations, and any other relevant factors when determining whether an employer is subject to undue hardship.[78] Presumably, larger organizations would be held to more stringent requirements for accommodating injured employees because these employers are more likely to have open positions that can be modified for employees with physical restrictions. Finally, those states that statutorily require employers to reinstate injured employees often allow employers to suspend or terminate disability benefits if the employee unreasonably refuses the job offer.[79]

Section 6.2.5
Required Job Search

A few jurisdictions have conditioned the receipt of workers' compensation benefits on whether the injured employee is conducting a job search or seeking suitable employment.[80] North Dakota provides that the "injured employee shall seek, obtain, and retain reasonable and substantial employment to reduce the period of temporary disability to a minimum. The employee has the burden of establishing that the employee has met this responsibility."[81] If the employee fails, without good cause, to make a good faith work search utilizing his transferable skills, then his disability and vocational rehabilitation benefits shall be suspended.[82]

Section 6.2.6

Preferred Worker Programs: Oregon's Return to Work Program

The state of Oregon is committed to bringing injured workers back to their jobs quickly and close to their pre-injury wages. Oregon accomplishes these goals in two distinct ways. First, like other states, the statute governing workers' compensation prohibits employers from discriminating against injured workers and entitles injured workers to reemployment.[83] Second, Oregon offers three return to work programs, which are designed specifically to engender early return to work with long term safety nets for injured workers.[84] Each program considers three fundamental pieces that work in harmony to create a successful return to work program: wage incentives, protection for the employer against re-injury, and reimbursement to the employer for costs associated with job modification for an injured employee.[85]

Workers' Benefit Fund

The Workers' Benefit Fund was created to fund Oregon's Reemployment Assistance Program, which includes the Employer-At-Injury Program and Preferred Worker Program, discussed more fully below.[86] The fund is financed by an assessment of 1.5 cents for each hour worked applied to employers and workers.[87] In 2006, the Workers' Benefit Fund expended $90.3 million.[88] This fund is crucial because it allows for the support of Oregon's unique programs.[89]

Employer-At-Injury Program[90]

This program provides financial incentives for employers to return injured workers to early-modified work.[91] Injured employees are eligible for the program if they have one or more restrictions that prevent employment at regular duty.[92] Employers receive a flat sixty dollar fee for EAIP placement. Furthermore, insurers reimburse employers in the form of wage subsidies up to 50 percent for up to three months and up to certain amounts for other expenses.[93] This program receives widespread praise from both employers and injured workers.[94]

Vocational Assistance Program

An injured worker is eligible for vocational assistance if he has a permanent disability that prevents him from obtaining employment in any job that pays 80 percent or more of the pre-injury wage.[95] Benefits under this program are similar to those of other states and can include maintenance indemnity payments during retraining, expenses for education, and rehabilitation services.[96] Generally, retraining is allowed for sixteen months (twenty-one months if necessary) in addition to four months of direct employment services.[97]

Preferred Worker Program

The primary purpose behind Oregon's Preferred Worker Program is to "encourage the re-employment of qualified Oregon workers who have permanent disabilities from on-the-job injury and who are not able to return to their regular employment because of those injuries."[98] This program is funded by the Workers' Benefit Fund.[99] The major program benefits include premium exceptions, claim cost reimbursement, and wage subsidies.[100] More specifically, under this program, an employer is not responsible for paying workers' compensation insurance premiums or premium assessments on a preferred worker for three years from the date of hire or eligibility.[101] Additionally, the employer may receive a 50 percent wage reimbursement for the preferred worker for 183 days.[102] Finally, the program provides assistance for employment purchases, up to certain maximum dollar amounts.[103] For example, the program provides for tuition, books, and fees; temporary lodging, meals, and mileage to attend instruction; tools and equipment; clothing; moving expenses; initiation fees; occupational certification; worksite creation costs; and worksite modification.[104]

An eligible worker would automatically receive a Preferred Worker Identification Card when the insurer or self-insurer reports that the employee has been released to restricted duty due to the compensable injury.[105] This card puts employers on notice that they may be entitled to the program's benefits if they employ such workers.[106] Ninety-two percent of respondents to a DCBS survey reported they would utilize the Preferred Worker Program again and found all aspects of the program useful.[107]

"Safety Net" For Workers Following Settlement

Finally, Oregon allows injured employees who have settled their claims an opportunity to take advantage of the Preferred Worker Program if they still require assistance obtaining employment.[108]

Section 6.3

Model Return to Work Practices

On January 22, 2009, a Congressman introduced H.R. 635 entitled "National Commission on State Workers' Compensation Laws Act of 2009" in order to establish the National Commission on State

Workers' Compensation Law.[109] Congressional findings showed that current state workers' compensation schemes might not be appropriate in light of "increases in medical knowledge, changes in the hazards associated with various employment, new risks to health and safety created by new technology, and increases in the general level of wages and in the cost of living."[110] The duties of the commission would entail studying and evaluating state workers' compensation laws to determine whether changes need to be made to accommodate the modern employer and injured employee.[111] The commission would also submit interim reports to the president and Congress detailing their findings, and making recommendations with regard to improvements in the state workers' compensation systems.[112] Previously, the same commission was established in 1972.

It is unclear whether The National Commission on State Workers' Compensation Laws would seek to federalize the workers' compensation system in order to provide uniformity in the field. Some have called for such a scheme and have questioned whether the state system is the best vehicle for resolving work injuries.[113] On the other hand, perhaps the commission will study each state's workers' compensation design and select the best aspects from the respective states to formulate the strongest return to work program. In order to draft a model policy, states must keep in mind the interests of both the employer and injured employee, and recognize that these goals are not incongruous. Both the employer and employee require incentives to make the transition back to work smooth and effective.

Section 6.3.1

Improving the Light Duty Job Offer

First, the use of the light duty job offer is the most widespread return to work program utilized by the states. While this scheme is effective in theory, the reality is that in many states the system can be manipulated to undue advantage. Employees in some states need only attempt to perform the job for a short period of time before they can claim they are incapacitated, thereby forcing employers to immediately recommence benefits, until a hearing can be had on the issue of whether the employee unjustifiably refused suitable light duty. For example, in Georgia a claimant may only attempt to work for an hour before he can claim an inability to do the job, and return home and continue to collect total disability benefits. The burden then shifts to the employer/insurer to request a hearing to address the issue of whether the employee can perform the work and is unjustifiably refusing the suitable light duty job. These provisions do not encourage the injured employee to keep trying to return to work, nor do they encourage the employer to offer light duty work.

An alternative approach would focus on requiring the injured employee to try to return to work more than once, for some reasonable grace period, before shifting the burden of proof to the employer/insurer to prove that the employee has unjustifiably refused suitable light work. For example, the employer would secure approval from the treating physician for a light duty job before he formally offers the job to the injured worker. Once the position is approved, the employee would have to return to work on a specified date and time as is customary in most states. The employer would be required to compensate the employee with temporary partial disability benefits, in addition to his salary, if there is a loss of income, while making an effort to perform the job. The employer/insurer would pay total disability lost time benefits for any full days of lost time due to a claimed inability to perform the light duty job during the grace period. If the employee reports for light duty the first week, but is unable to perform, he must see the treating physician again, and if released to do light work, he must come back the following week to try again. His lost time disability benefits would continue. If the employee returns the following week and again claims he cannot work, the process begins anew. If after a certain period of time, about a month, for example, the injured employee has made several good faith attempts to return to work to no avail, then the employer must recommence total disability benefits, subject to their right to request a hearing to determine whether the injured employee has unjustifiably refused suitable work. The employee is compensated to try to work, his lost time benefits continue while he is trying to return to work, and the employer is given another chance to return his employee to suitable employment. On the other hand, if the employee does not attempt to perform the job at all, on any of the scheduled times during the proscribed period of time, the employer may unilaterally suspend his lost time benefits, subject to the employee's right to request a hearing to determine whether he has justifiably refused light duty. At that time, the burden would then shift to the injured worker to demonstrate ongoing disability. Pending the hearing, the parties would be required to participate in a mediation to try to resolve the return to work issues. The mediation would be given a high priority by the board or commission, which would schedule expedited mediations, and hearings on return to work issues. This system would encourage honesty, and take into account the needs of both the employer and injured worker.

In the alternative, states could adopt a modified version of Georgia's current light duty job offer program. If the authorized treating physician released the employee to return to work with restrictions, and the employer offered a suitable light duty job, the employee would be required to attempt the proffered job during a fifteen scheduled work day grace period. The injured employee would be compensated while working during the trial return to work period with temporary partial disability benefits, to at least partially compensate him for any loss of income. If, during that period, the injured employee was unable to perform the job for the entire fifteen scheduled work days, the parties would be required to mediate the return to work issue. The board or commission would give it priority and schedule an expedited mediation. If the parties were unable to reach an agreement in mediation, the employer/insurer would have the opportunity to request an expedited hearing to address the return to work issue. Although Georgia law places the burden of proof on the employer/insurer where the employee claims an inability to perform the light duty job within the fifteen day grace period, under this proposed alternative approach, the burden of proof would be shifted to the injured worker to demonstrate ongoing disability such that he could not perform the light duty job. If a judge determined the injured worker could not, in fact, perform the light duty job, the employer/insurer would have to immediately recommence total disability benefits.

By the same token, providing temporary alternative or transitional work opportunities is another effective tool in bringing injured employees back to work. As stated above, those who remain out of work for extended periods of time often never return. Though some employers may not have temporary positions available, experts recommend sending an injured employee elsewhere to work at a local charity, for example.[114] Transitional work has been shown to save claims costs. In Ohio, a Bureau of Workers' Compensation study showed that employers who used a transitional work program saved $1,108 on average in compensation claim costs and an average of $139 in medical costs per claim.[115] Those employers were also able to return injured workers to the job ten days sooner than employers who did not utilize a transitional work program.[116]

States that currently mandate temporary alternative work opportunities do not allow the employee the chance to justifiably refuse the offer and continue to collect disability benefits. Rather, the statutes appear to unconditionally permit the employer to request a reduction or termination of compensation if the employee refuses the work. So, unlike the light duty job offer, this provision provides a stronger financial incentive for the employee to return to work.

Section 6.3.2

The Carrot and Stick: Mandatory Employee Reinstatement and Premium Discounts

Compelling employers to reinstate injured workers where there is work available to which the employee could be assigned could work well in conjunction with premium discounts or dividends. That is to say, employers would have the burden to make room for injured workers only where such an arrangement is reasonably feasible for the employer. Employers would be held accountable because they would face monetary penalties for failure to comply. At the same time, employees are discouraged from refusing the offer for fear their lost time disability benefits will be suspended. However, just as the light duty job offer may promote dishonesty on the part of the injured employee, this statutory provision may allow employers to further stall the return to work process. More specifically, employers may be reluctant to bring injured employees back to work because they worry that injured employees will display poor attitude problems, which will in turn lead to decreased productivity and morale amongst other employees. Employers may also experience anxiety at the thought of returning an injured employee to work for fear that the employee will sustain a new injury or aggravate his prior injury. Saddling employers with a negative financial incentive may further exacerbate the already tense situation. If employers decrease their costs by returning injured workers to suitable employment, perhaps a tangible reward is in order. In order to sweeten the arrangement for employers, states could adopt Colorado's policy of providing a premium dividend of up to 10 percent if an employer re-employs injured employees at their pre-injury wages. Using reinstatement rights and premium dividends together ensures that the employer and injured employee get something out of the deal, and the ultimate goal of returning the employee to suitable employment at his pre-injury wages is accomplished.

Section 6.3.3

Ensuring the "Job Search" is Effectively Performed

In the alternative, if it is not feasible for employers to return injured workers to light duty jobs, or if the employee is physically unable to return to available modified employment with his former employer, states could enact statutory provisions to mandate that employees conduct continuing good faith job searches, within their physical restrictions, in order to continue to be eligible for disability benefits. This would be similar to the ongoing job searches required to collect unemployment insurance. States like Ohio and North Dakota currently require job searches as a condition to the receipt of disability benefits.[117]

However, job searches are not customarily required to continue after the employee is awarded lost time total disability benefits, even where the employee is subsequently released by his physician to restricted duty work. Furthermore, job searches are often relegated to mere formality whereby employees simply provide the right answers to questions or go through the motions without really looking for suitable work.[118] In order for job searches to have any value as a return to work program, states must require specific evidence to show that employees are in fact making a good faith search for work within their physical restrictions.

First and foremost, the burden of proving a sufficient job search must be on the employee. States could require more specific evidence of the job search, to assure that it is done effectively and in good faith. For example, states could demand more evidence of the steps the employee took to complete a good faith work search, such as the number of employment applications, whether job interviews were in person or over the phone or online, and whether employees revealed their restrictions to potential employers in order to satisfy their burden that they were unable to obtain suitable employment because of their job injury.

Court supervision of the job search would be another alternative to assure that the employee continues to look for suitable work, in exchange for his continued receipt of lost time disability benefits. Court supervision could be accomplished primarily in two ways, by vocational rehabilitation and/or hearings. Rehabilitation counselors have long been used in the workers' compensation system to assist employees in finding work within their physical restrictions. States could have mandatory periodic status hearings to ensure that injured employees are actively looking for work. For example, the first hearing could occur three months after the date the employee was released to light duty work. If at that time the employee proved he was unable to obtain employment within his work-related restrictions, he would be entitled to continue to receive temporary total disability benefits. These status hearings could be held every three months until fifty-two aggregate weeks had expired from the date the employee was released to light duty work. At that time, if the employee was still unable to obtain suitable employment, the employer would be able to reduce his total disability lost time benefits to temporary partial benefits. Even after the injured worker's benefits are reduced to temporary partial levels, he would have to continue to prove an ongoing viable job search at status hearings. However, once the employee's benefits have been reduced, the status hearings could be held every six months. If at any time an injured worker fails to look for suitable work, employers would be entitled to unilaterally suspend benefits until the following status hearing. This result would ensure that employees take a proactive role in returning to the work force.

Section 6.3.4

Medical and Vocational Rehabilitation: Improving the Mind and Body

Of course, in many instances returning an employee to work following a job injury is not only a matter of providing legal and financial incentives to employers and employees. An injured worker typically has some loss of bodily function that may prevent him from returning to his former job, or at the very least prevents him from returning for some period of time. Therefore, both medical and vocational rehabilitation services are critical to bringing a healthy employee back to the workplace. Arguably, these services must be utilized together in order to facilitate the best result. For example, states that emphasize medical recovery but fail to employ vocational rehabilitation may be extending the period of time an employee remains out of work. The employee will continue to receive medical benefits even after he returns to work. However, employers may reduce or even terminate disability benefits when an employee goes back to work. Those states that mandate vocational services make it clear that employers must provide the injured employee with the opportunity to return to gainful employment in order to reduce their indemnity exposure. By expending resources to return the employee to work, either with the former employer or with a new employer, employers can reduce their costs exponentially in the long run.

Section 6.3.5

Lessons from Oregon: An Innovative System

Finally, state legislators across the United States have studied the Oregon scheme when considering improving their respective workers' compensation systems.[119] One study conducted by the RAND Institute for Civil Justice compared the median number of days off following a work injury and found that at thirty-eight days, Oregon's median number of days was slightly longer than Wisconsin (thirty-six days), shorter than Washington (forty-five days), but significantly shorter than New Mexico (seventy-seven days).[120] This information lends some credence to the strength of Oregon's return to work system. While lessons can be gleaned from the structure in Oregon, the Workers' Compensation Research Institute warns that a process that is successful in one state may not provide the same results in another.[121]

Though Oregon has enacted return to work provisions that are similar to other states, it also has special programs unlike any other state. Both the Employer-At-Injury and Preferred Worker Programs provide incentives to employers and employees to encourage early return to work. As stated above, system participants stated they were pleased with the programs and would recommend them to other states. Under an Employer-At-Injury program, employers would receive significant wage subsidies for returning employees to early-modified work. These allowances could assist the employer with the various costs associated with bringing an injured worker back to work, such as work site modifications, tools and equipment, clothing, and other expenses. By the same token, the Preferred Worker Program works somewhat like the former second injury funds in that it would encourage employers to hire employees who have sustained prior injuries that prevent them from returning to their former jobs. However, unlike second injury funds, the Preferred Worker Program would provide multiple financial incentives to employers, such as insurance premium discounts and wage subsidies. Perhaps more importantly, injured workers would be given a second chance in the workplace and would be provided with sufficient education and training to ensure they are successful in their new jobs. Finally, states could offer employees more assistance even after they have settled their claims in the form of continued eligibility for the Preferred Worker Program.

Section 6.4

Conclusion

No legal solution can take the place of employers, employees, insurance adjusters, physicians, and attorneys working together to facilitate the return to work process. However, many of the suggestions above contemplate rehabilitating the mind and body to bring the injured employee back to work by providing incentives to ease frustrations, provide financial assistance in times of need, requiring the employee to make a continuing job search for work within his physical restrictions, and placing some responsibility on the employer to help the employee get back on his feet. Likewise, these same statutory provisions recognize that employers need assistance and should be rewarded for their efforts in bringing the injured back to work. By striking a balance between the interests of the employer and those of the employee, states can more effectively govern the return to work process.

---

[1] *See* Margaret Spence, *Return to Work Program 101: The Grim Statistics 80 Billion Lost Work Days Due to Injury or Illness*, AM. CHRONICLE, Apr. 15, 2008, http://www.americanchronicle.com/articles/view/58555 (examining the effect injury and illness have on the workforce). Margaret Spence is a "Board Certified Workers' Compensation consultant, speaker, and trainer who ranks among the experts in the field of Injury Management and Return to Work Implementation." *Id.*

[2] *Id.*

[3] *Id.*

⁴ *See* Jim Barlow, HOUSTON CHRONICLE, Oct. 31, 2000, *available at* 2000 WLNR 6361505 (stating that companies that make the effort to design and implement light duty work for injured workers "wind up with improved morale, more productivity and a better work force"). *But see* WORKERS' COMP. GUIDE § 6:4 (West, Westlaw through Aug. 2008) (stating that if employers return injured employees to the workplace early they can reduce medical claim costs by 15–20% and can save 80–100% of lost wages costs).

⁵ Barlow, *supra* note 4 and accompanying text.

⁶ *See* WORKERS' COMP. GUIDE, *supra* note 4, at § 6:4 (reporting that employees who do not return to work within 90 days of injury have less than a 50% chance of ever returning, and employees who do not return to work within 120 days of injury have less than a 10% chance of returning to any job).

⁷ *Id.*

⁸ *Id.*

⁹ Spence, *supra* note 1 and accompanying text.

¹⁰ *Id.*

¹¹ *Id. See also* 43% of Employers Don't Have a Return-to-Work Program, Says Poll at www.reduceyourworkerscomp.com, http://www.reuters.com/article/pressRelease/idUS181841+20-Oct-2008+MW20081020 (last visited Jan. 18, 2009) (stating that only 57% of employers who answered a poll reported having a return to work program designed to bring injured employees back to work quickly).

¹² *See* Rob O'Regan, *A Return-to-Work Program Can Ease the Sting of Worker Compensation*, EXPERT BUS. SOURCE, Apr. 18, 2007, http://www.expertbusinesssource.com/article/CA6434721.html (providing four suggestions for enacting a successful return to work program).

¹³ *See* Margaret Spence, *Can Injured Employees Return to Work? Successfully?*, July 30, 2008, http://workerscompgazette.com/can-injured-employees-return to work-successfully/ (contending that effective return to work policies are implemented before the employee is injured).

¹⁴ *Id.*

¹⁵ Approximately thirty-nine states provide that temporary total disability benefits can be terminated if an employee refuses an offer of suitable employment. Such states include, but are not limited to, Alabama, Arkansas, Colorado, Delaware, Florida, Indiana, Iowa, Maine, Michigan, Minnesota, Montana, New Mexico, North Carolina, South Carolina, Tennessee, and Virginia.

¹⁶ Note that Alabama, Arkansas, Delaware, Florida, Indiana, North Carolina, South Carolina, and Virginia, among others, have statutes similar to or identical to Georgia. However, unlike other states, Georgia does allow a claimant to recover any Permanent Partial Disability (PPD) benefits to which he may be entitled during the period he refuses a suitable job offer from his employer.

¹⁷ LARSON'S WORKERS' COMP. LAW § 85.01 (2008).

¹⁸ *See* State Board of Worker's Compensation Form WC-240(a).

¹⁹ Georgia Board Rule 240(b)(2)(i).

²⁰ *City of Adel v. Wise*, 261 Ga. 53, 401 S.E.2d 522 (1991).

²¹ *See Martines v. Worley & Sons Construc.*, 278 Ga. App. 26, 628 S.E.2d 113 (2006), *cert. denied* (Sept. 8, 2006).

²² *Id.*

²³ *Id.*

²⁴ GA. CODE. ANN. § 34-9-240(b)(2) (West 2008); Board Rule 240(b)(3).

²⁵ *City of Adel v. Wise*, 261 Ga. 53, 56, 401 S.E.2d 522 (1991).

²⁶ *Id.*

²⁷ *Id.*

28 *Clark v. Georgia Kraft Co.*, 178 Ga. App. 884, 345 S.E.2d 61 (1986).

29 *See City of Adel v. Wise*, 261 Ga. 53 (1991) (citing *Acco-Babcock, Inc. v. Counts*, 1988 WL 31967 (Superior Court of Delaware, 1988)).

30 *See McDaniel v. Roper Corp.*, 149 Ga. App. 864, 256 S.E.2d 146 (1979) (holding that an employee could not refuse employment within her restrictions because she did not want to work second shift).

31 N.C. GEN. STAT. ANN. § 97-32.1 (West 2008).

32 *Id.*

33 *Id.*

34 GA. CODE. ANN. § 34-9-240(b)(1) (West 2008). Note, the employer may then file a hearing request to contest the reinstatement of benefits.

35 *See* N.H. REV. STAT. ANN. § 281-A:23-b (2008) ("All employers with 5 or more employees shall develop temporary alternative work opportunities for injured employees. If the employee fails to accept temporary alternative work, the employer may petition . . . to reduce or end compensation. Notwithstanding . . . if an injured employee returns to temporary alternative work within 5 days of sustaining the injury, such employee shall be paid workers' compensation from the first date of injury").

36 For an overview of this return to work scheme *see* New Hampshire Department of Labor, http://www.labor.state.nh.us/injured_worker_temporary_duty.asp?ptype=text (last visited Feb. 7, 2009) (emphasizing the importance of physicians, employers, and adjusters working together to bring the injured employee back to work).

37 *Id.*

38 *Id.*

39 *Id.*

40 *Id.*

41 *Id.*

42 COLO. REV. STAT. ANN. § 8-42-107.6 (West 2008).

43 For an overview of each state's rehabilitation scheme, *see* Rehabilitation Benefits Provided For Injured Workers Under State Workers' Compensation Laws, http://www.scribd.com/doc/1710183/Department-of-Labor-table15 (last visited Feb. 15, 2009).

44 HAW. REV. STAT. § 386-25 (2008).

45 *See* WORKERS' COMP. GUIDE, *supra* note 4, at § 6:21 (noting that it makes logical sense to rehabilitate and retain an existing employee than to recruit and train a new employee).

46 *Id.*

47 States such as Hawaii, Illinois, Iowa, Kansas, Kentucky, Louisiana, Maine, Michigan, Minnesota, Missouri, Montana, Nevada, New Hampshire, New York, North Dakota, Oklahoma, Oregon, Rhode Island, South Dakota, Utah and Vermont, among others, have some sort of rehabilitation program to assist injured workers in returning to work.

48 WORKERS' COMP. GUIDE, *supra* note 4, at § 6:18.

49 *Id.*

50 *Id. See* N.H. REV. STAT. ANN. §281-A:25 (2008) ("If an employee refuses to accept vocational rehabilitation . . . the employee may lose compensation for each week of the refusal").

51 WORKERS' COMP. GUIDE, *supra* note 4, at § 6:18.

52 *Id.*

53 *See* New York State Workers' Compensation Board, http://www.wcb.state.ny.us/content/main/workers/rehab.jsp (last visited Feb. 8, 2009).

54 *See* WORKERS' COMP. GUIDE, *supra* note 4, at § 6:17 (outlining the differences between medical and vocational rehabilitation).

55 *See* State of New Jersey, Department of Labor and Workforce Development, http://lwd.state.nj.us/labor/wc/content/oscf.html (last visited Feb. 7, 2009).

56 *Id.*

57 HAW. REV. STAT. § 386-25 (2008). *See also* KAN. STAT. ANN. § 44-510g (2008) ("No vocational assessment, evaluation, services or training shall be provided or made available under the workers' compensation act unless specifically agreed to by the employer or insurance carrier providing or making available such assessment, evaluation, services or training"); Mo. Rev. Stat.§ 287.148 (West 2008) ("If the employer can determine that a loss of suitable, gainful employment has occurred, the employer may retain the services of a rehabilitation practitioner or a rehabilitation provider"); NEV. REV. STAT. ANN. § 616C.550 ("If benefits . . . will be paid to an injured employee for more than 90 days, the insurer or the injured employee may request a vocational rehabilitation counselor").

58 HAW. REV. STAT. § 386-25 (2008).

59 *Id.*

60 *Id.*

61 KY. REV. STAT. ANN. § 342.710 (West 2008).

62 *Id.*

63 IOWA CODE ANN. § 85.70 (West 2008).

64 *Id.*

65 States like Alaska, Arkansas, Colorado, Connecticut, Georgia, Illinois, Iowa, Kansas, Louisiana, Maryland, Mississippi, Missouri, North Carolina, Oklahoma, South Carolina, and Tennessee, among others, have developed second injury funds. For a typical second injury fund statute, *see* S.C. CODE ANN. § 42-9-400 which reads:

[i]f an employee who has a permanent physical impairment from any cause or origin incurs a subsequent disability from injury by accident arising out of and in the course of his employment, resulting in compensation and medical payments liability or either, for disability that is substantially greater and is caused by aggravation of the preexisting impairment than that which would have resulted from the subsequent injury alone, the employer or his insurance carrier shall pay all awards of compensation and medical benefits provided by this title; but such employer or his insurance carrier shall be reimbursed from the Second Injury Fund . . . for compensation and medical benefits.

66 *See* State of New Jersey, Department of Labor and Workforce Development, http://lwd.state.nj.us/labor/wc/content/oscf.html (last visited Feb. 7, 2009).

67 *See* WORKERS' COMP. GUIDE, *supra* note 4, at § 1:32 (discussing the history of second injury funds and their purpose).

68 *Id.*

69 *Id.*

70 *See Louisiana Workers' Comp. Corp. v. Louisiana Workers' Comp. Second Injury Bd.*, 1996-0808 (La. App. 1 Cir. 2/14/97); 691 So.2d 122 (discussing the requirements for reimbursement by the second injury fund).

71 5-91 LARSON'S WORKERS' COMP. LAW § 91.03(8) (2005).

72 *Id.*

73 *Id.*

74 *See* GA. CODE ANN. § 34-9-368 ("The Subsequent Injury Trust Fund shall not reimburse a self-insured employer or an insurer for a subsequent injury for which a claim is made for an injury occurring after June 30, 2006").

75 ARK. CODE ANN. § 11-9-505(a)(1) (West 2008). *See also* CONN. GEN. STAT. ANN. § 31-313(c) (West 2008) (providing that "[w]henever the commissioner finds that an employer has failed to comply . . . he may assess a civil penalty of not more than five hundred dollars against the employer"); N.H. REV. STAT. ANN. § 281-A:25-a (2008) ("[t]he commissioner may assess employers in

violation . . . all weekly wage benefits retroactive to the date the injured employee was eligible for reinstatement"); N.M. STAT. ANN. § 52-1-50.1 (West 2008) ("[t]he exclusive remedy for a violation . . . shall be a fine").

[76] ME. REV. STAT. ANN. TIT. 39-A § 218 (2008). *See also* N.H. REV. STAT. ANN. § 281-A:25-a (2008), *supra* note 36 (the right to reinstatement expires if a medical practitioner determines the employee cannot return to work, the employee accepts employment with a different employer, or *eighteen months from the date of injury*) (emphasis added).

[77] ME. REV. STAT. ANN. TIT. 39-A § 218 (2008).

[78] *Id.*

[79] For example, in Arkansas, though the employer must provide a modified job for an injured employee, where such job is available, if the employee refuses the job offer, he shall not be entitled to compensation during the period of refusal unless it was justifiable. ARK. CODE ANN. § 11-9-526 (West 2008). *See also* ME. REV. STAT. ANN. TIT. 39-A § 218 (2008) ("If an injured employee refuses to accept an offer of reinstatement for a position suitable to the employee's physical condition, the employee is considered to have voluntarily withdrawn from the work force and is no longer entitled to any wage loss benefits . . . during the period of refusal").

[80] *See* N.D. CENT. CODE § 65.05.1-04 (2008) (requiring an injured worker to conduct a job search).

[81] *Id.*

[82] *Id.*

[83] *See Lessons From the Oregon Workers' Compensation System*, 24 WORKERS' COMP. RESEARCH INST. 1, at 6 (Mar. 2008).

[84] *Id.* at 6–7.

[85] *Id.* at 7.

[86] *Id.*

[87] *Id.*

[88] *Id.*

[89] *Id.*

[90] For more information on the Employer-At-Injury Program *see* The employer-at-injury program (EAIP), http://www.cbs.state.or.us/external/wcd/rdrs/rau/eaip/eaip_overview.html (last visited Feb. 9, 2009) (discussing the benefits of the EAIP).

[91] *See Lessons From the Oregon Workers' Compensation System, supra* note 83, at 7.

[92] *Id.*

[93] *Id.*

[94] *Id.*

[95] *Id.* at 8.

[96] *Id.*

[97] *Id.*

[98] *See* Oregon Preferred Worker Program, http://www.cbs.state.or.us/external/wcd/communications/publications/3077.pdf (last visited Feb. 9, 2009) (outlining the Preferred Worker Program).

[99] *Id.*

[100] *Id.*

[101] *Id.*

[102] *Id.*

[103] *Id.*

[104] *Id.*

[105] *See Lessons From the Oregon Workers' Compensation System, supra* note 83, at 8.

[106] *Id.*

[107] *Id.*

[108] *Id.*

[109] National Commission on State Workers' Compensation Laws Act of 2009, H.R. 635, 111th Cong. (2009).

[110] *Id.* at § 2(3).

[111] *Id.* at § 4.

[112] *Id.* at § 8(a).

[113] For an overview of federal reform in the workers' compensation field *see* Joan T.A. Gabel, Article, *Escalating Inefficiency in Workers' Compensation Systems: Is Federal Reform the Answer?*, 34 WAKE FOREST L. REV. 1083 (1999) (positing that state workers' compensation systems are inconsistent and inefficient so a federal approach may be the solution). Further, she argues that "[t]he state by state approach to workers' compensation has resulted in varying state judicial exceptions and widely ranging benefits levels. These discrepancies interfere with the goals of uniformity, efficiency, fairness, and predictability in our workers' compensation system." *Id.* at 1111.

[114] *See* Rebecca Shafer Bruce, *Taking the Sting Out of Comp Costs*, 563 PLI/LIT 137, 165 (1997) (discussing suggestions for successful return to work programs).

[115] Ohio.gov, Bureau of Workers' Compensation: Transitional Work, http://www.ohiobwc.com/employer/programs/transworkgrant/twghome.asp (last visited Feb. 15, 2009).

[116] *Id.*

[117] N.D. CENT. CODE § 65-05.1-04 (2008).

[118] *See* Edward M. Welch, *Statutory Provisions That Encourage Return-To-Work*.

[119] *See Lessons From the Oregon Workers' Compensation System, supra* note 83, at 1.

[120] *Id.* at 7.

[121] *Id.* at 1.

Chapter 7
Coordination of Benefits

THE INTERPLAY BETWEEN WORKERS' COMPENSATION, THE AMERICANS WITH DISABILITIES ACT, AND THE FAMILY MEDICAL LEAVE ACT

This chapter was taken from the *Georgia Worker's Compensation Desk Manual* authored by Mike Bagley and John Ferguson. The chapter on coordination of benefits was authored by Joe Chancey and Leigh Lawson Reeves (who is now deceased). All are (were) partners with Drew, Eckl, and Farnham in Atlanta, Georgia. You can get the complete copy of the *Georgia Worker's Compensation Desk Manual* at www.gwca.info.

Section 7.1
Introduction

With the advent of the Americans with Disabilities Act (ADA) in 1992 and The Family and Medical Leave Act (FMLA) in 1993, the ways in which employers were required to assess their handling of workers' compensation claims changed dramatically. Prior to the ADA and FMLA, if an individual was injured on the job, employers in many states could simply choose to terminate that individual, with no real employment consequences. Moreover, prior to hiring an individual, the employer could specifically ask the employee about pre-existing medical conditions and past work injuries. Now, while job-related information may be gleaned about an employee's past and current medical conditions, employers must obtain this information only after a conditional job offer has been made and prior to an employee actually starting work. The employer must also seek the same information from all applicants within the same job classification.

Recently, both the ADA and FMLA have also been amended, and the primary purpose and effect of the amendments has been to expand the rights given to employees. The ADA was amended effective January 1, 2009, and the most significant change was an expansion of the definition of a "disability." As a result, many more employees will now be considered to be "disabled" and able to exercise rights under the ADA. Similarly, the FMLA regulations were amended effective January 16, 2009, to expand the leave rights granted to employees. Consequently, employers must consider the ADA and FMLA in deciding how to deal with employees with medical conditions.

The most important thing for employers to remember is that the Georgia Workers' Compensation Act, ADA, and FMLA are *not* mutually exclusive. It is possible (and not at all unusual) for an employee to be covered by all three laws simultaneously. Stated another way, an employee who has suffered a compensable workers' compensation injury may also qualify as having a "disability" under the ADA and a "serious health condition" under the FMLA. Therefore, in dealing with an employee who has a workers' compensation claim, the employer should not lose sight of the fact that the employee may also have rights under one or both of the federal laws.

Section 7.2

Covered Employers

Section 7.2.1

Workers' Compensation

While the criteria for coverage under workers' compensation laws vary from state to state, the majority of employers will be subject to workers' compensation insurance requirements. The original purpose of workers' compensation laws was to provide a portion of lost wages and medical care for persons injured on the job. It is typically a no-fault recovery system and each state has its own separate laws which govern the requirements of each employer and employee. The primary focus is usually whether a work injury "arises out of and in the course and scope of employment."

Section 7.2.2
Americans with Disabilities Act

The ADA applies to employers with fifteen or more employees for each working day in each of twenty or more calendar weeks in the current or preceding calendar year. Under the ADA, state and local governments are considered employers for purposes of the ADA, regardless of the number of employees working for the government entity at any given time.

The purpose of the ADA is to prohibit discrimination against persons with disabilities with respect to their employment. Title I of the ADA covers not only current employees, but also applicants for employment, and specifically provides protection to any "qualified individuals with a disability."[1]

Section 7.2.3
Family and Medical Leave Act

Under the FMLA, employers that employ fifty or more employees for at least twenty work weeks during the current or preceding calendar year are covered employers under the Act. Moreover, state and local governments are employers as defined under the FMLA, no matter how many employees are working for the government entity at any given time.

In general, FMLA requires employers to provide employees up to twelve weeks of unpaid leave in certain medical and/or family situations. The employer must also continue to keep the employee's job protected and available for their return. If the employee's specific job cannot remain vacant for twelve weeks, the employer must provide the employee with a position which is substantially similar to the original job upon their return.[2]

Section 7.3
Covered Employees

Section 7.3.1
Workers' Compensation

The term "employee" under workers' compensation laws generally refers to any person in the service of another unless the employment is not in the usual course of business. Workers' compensation laws in some states also include some workers who might not necessarily be considered traditional employees, such as minors, volunteer firefighters, police officers, etc. Applicable workers' compensation law must be considered to determine whether an individual is covered.

Section 7.3.2
Americans with Disabilities Act

As noted above, the ADA is different from both the Workers' Compensation Act and the FMLA, in that it covers not only current employees, but also applicants for employment. Moreover, individuals with a current disability, those with a history of a disability, or those who are simply "regarded by others as having a disability" are protected by the ADA if they are also considered "qualified" for the positions.[3] Persons defined as having a "disability" are those who have a physical or mental impairment that substantially limits one or more major life activities.[4] To be a "qualified" individual under the ADA, the employee must have the requisite skill, experience, and education, and other job-related requirements for the employment position and be capable of performing the "essential functions" of the job, with or without reasonable accommodation.[5]

Section 7.3.3
Family and Medical Leave Act

An employee is eligible for FMLA leave only if they have worked for the employer for at least twelve months and have worked at least 1,250 hours during the twelve-month period immediately preceding the request for leave. If the employee meets these qualifications and suffers from a "serious health condition," as defined by the FMLA, the employee is entitled to a total of twelve work weeks of leave during a twelve-month period.[6] (The FMLA also gives the employee right to leave: (1) to provide care for an immediate family member who is suffering a "serious health condition," (2) due to the birth, adoption, or placement of a child with the employee; or (3) for certain military-related purposes.)

Section 7.4
"Disability" vs. "Serious Health Condition"

The most important part of considering how these pieces of legislation interact is to first determine whether an individual who sustains a compensable work injury may be entitled to protection under the ADA or the FMLA. As such, it is imperative to have a good working knowledge of what constitutes a "disability" under the Workers' Compensation Act and the ADA, and what constitutes a "serious health condition" under the FMLA. It is important to remember that each workers' compensation case must be analyzed on an individual basis.

Section 7.4.1
Workers' Compensation/Disability

In general, conditions considered to constitute injuries for the purpose of workers' compensation claims are those that "arise out of and in the course of the employment relationship."[7] Such injuries may include temporary or permanent conditions, aggravation of pre-existing problems, repetitive trauma injuries, mental problems, and even occupational disease. Thus, a wide range of illnesses and injuries fall under the scope of the Workers' Compensation Act.

Section 7.4.2

Americans with Disabilities Act/Disability

In contrast, the Americans with Disabilities Act (ADA) has specific requirements to determine whether a person is "qualified" for the job, and if so, if he or she has a true "disability." Specifically, the ADA prohibits discrimination against (1) a qualified individual (2) with a disability (3) who can perform the essential functions of the job (4) with or without reasonable accommodation.

"Qualified Individual"

Essentially, under the ADA, a "qualified individual" must have the requisite skill, experience, education, and other job-related requirements of an employment position and be capable of performing the "essential functions of the job" with or without reasonable accommodation.[8] Consequently, one of the first decisions to be addressed in determining whether a workers' compensation claim might be covered under the ADA is to see whether the worker who is injured is considered a "qualified" individual under the ADA.

This concept was illustrated in the case of *Browning v. Liberty Mutual Insurance Co.*, in which the plaintiff, Browning, had been diagnosed with cubital tunnel syndrome. She went on workers' compensation leave and had surgery to correct the problem.[9] After the surgery, she returned to work on a part-time basis, with reduced responsibilities and a variety of other accommodations. After working in this light-duty job for a few days, Browning ceased working altogether, contending that she was experiencing increased pain in her arm and hand, which prohibited her from performing her light-duty job. She did not call in as required by the company's attendance policy, and was terminated on the grounds of job abandonment. Soon thereafter, she commenced an action based on alleged violations of the ADA and the FMLA.

After trial, the jury found for Browning on her ADA claim and awarded damages. However, the Eighth Circuit reversed the jury award for Browning, and instead, found that, given her limitations when she returned to work, she was not considered a "qualified individual" under the ADA at the time of her termination. The court stated:

The ADA is broad in its scope, but it only protects individuals who can perform their job. The plaintiff was terminated while recovering from her injury, and prior to the point in her recovery when she could once again perform the essential functions of her job. The fact that she continued to heal, gaining strength and use of her arm, once again becoming a qualified individual who could perform the essential functions of the job, does not obviate the fact that she was not a qualified individual at the time of her termination and, thus, not under the protective umbrella of the ADA.

Although not involving a work injury, the case of *Robertson v. Neuromedical Center*, further illustrates the analysis most courts apply in analyzing whether a worker is deemed "qualified" under the ADA.[10]

Specifically, in *Robertson* a neurologist who had diagnosed himself as suffering from attention deficit hyperactivity disorder (ADHD) was terminated from his position at the hospital because he was not completing reports on his patients in a timely manner. Following his termination, the neurologist filed suit under the ADA, arguing that the employer had unlawfully discriminated against him based upon his disability. Because the court found that performing administrative tasks was an essential function of the job of a neurologist, they held that the physician was not "qualified" for the position he held, and as such, his termination did not violate the ADA.

"Disability"

Assuming the individual injured on the job is deemed "qualified," they must still be considered "disabled" under the ADA. The ADA defines a "disabled" person as someone with (1) a physical and mental impairment (2) that substantially limits (3) a major life activity. As noted above, an individual is also protected under the ADA if they are simply regarded as having such an impairment.[11]

The definition of a disability was one of the most important points of focus of the Americans with Disabilities Act Amendments Act of 2008 ("ADAAA"). Specifically, the ADAAA changed significant parts of the definition of a "disability," in order to provide broader coverage to a larger percentage of the population. The ADAAA was motivated by many years of judicial decisions that had interpreted the ADA very narrowly, and that had specifically imposed strict limitations on the definition of "disability." As a result, the ADAAA has created important changes that have effectively reversed almost two decades of case law. It may be helpful to briefly review some of the cases that led to the passage of the ADAAA, which have been "undone" by the new legislation.

An example of such a case was *Toyota Motor Manufacturing Kentucky, Inc. v. Williams*.[12] In the *Toyota* case, the plaintiff suffered from carpal tunnel syndrome resulting in manual task limitations. As a result, she was terminated from her assembly line production job. The Court held that although she was terminated due to her physical limitations, she was not "disabled" as defined in the ADA unless she was able to prove that she was unable to perform "the variety of tasks central to most people's daily lives, not whether the claimant is unable to perform the tasks associated with her particular job." In other words, just because this particular claimant was unable to perform her assembly line duties, it did not mean she was substantially limited in the major life activity of working. The *Toyota* case therefore stood for the proposition that the inability to physically perform a particular job did not establish a disability.

The courts had also decided that a person should not be considered disabled if their medical limitation could be remedied or controlled by some corrective measures. Specifically, in *Sutton v. United Airlines, Inc.*, twin sisters were denied the opportunity to interview for positions as commercial pilots when it was discovered that their uncorrected visual acuity was 20/200 or worse.[13] When their vision deficiency was uncovered, their interviews were terminated, and the twins filed a charge of discrimination under the ADA. The United States Supreme Court recognized that, with corrective measures (eyeglasses), the twins' vision was 20/20 or better. Accordingly, the Court held that an individual whose physical or mental impairment is controlled by mitigating measures does not have an impairment that substantially limits that individual from a major life activity. Consequently, the twins were found not to be "disabled" under the provisions of the ADA.

The ADAAA took dead aim at the *Toyota* and *Sutton* decisions, and imposed changes to the existing statute that specifically reversed their results. First, the ADAAA changed the definition of a "disability," making it clear that any doubts should be resolved in favor of extending ADA rights. The ADAAA states that the definition of disability "shall be construed in favor of broad coverage of individuals under this Act, to the maximum extent permitted by the terms of this Act." It also stated that the EEOC's regulatory definition of "substantially limits" was overly strict.

The ADAAA retains the terms "substantially limits" and "major life activities" from the original ADA definition of "disability," but makes clear that the limitations imposed by previous Supreme Court cases would no longer apply. In that regard, the ADAAA specifically catalogues numerous examples of "major life activities" that must be substantially limited in order for an impairment to be a disability, rather than leaving that phrase open to interpretation. The non-exhaustive list of major life activities in includes caring for oneself, performing manual tasks, seeing, hearing, eating, sleeping, walking, standing, lifting, bending, speaking, breathing, learning, reading, concentrating, thinking, communicating, and working. The ADAAA also lists *major bodily functions*, including, but not limited to, functions of the immune system; normal cell growth; and digestive, bowel, bladder, neurological, brain, respiratory, circulatory, endocrine, and reproductive functions.

The ADAAA also specifically rejected the *Sutton* decision. It prohibits employers from considering mitigating measures such as medication, assistive technology, accommodations, or modifications when determining whether an impairment substantially limits a major life activity. In other words, if an individual would be disabled without prescribed medications, assistive devices, or other available measures, that individual qualifies for protection under the ADA, even if they would not qualify as disabled with such medical assistance. The ADAAA also provides that impairments that are episodic or in remission are to be assessed in their active state.

Finally, the ADAAA made it easier for a person to establish a claim for being "regarded as" disabled. The law now requires only that an individual show that he or she has been subjected to an action prohibited under the Act because of an actual or perceived physical or mental impairment that is "not transitory and minor." A claimant is no longer required to prove that he or she suffers, or was regarded by the employer as suffering, a condition that limits a major life activity. Simply stated, if an employer takes an adverse action against an employee due to a physical or medical condition, it is likely that it will violate the "regarded as" provision of the ADAAA, even if the employee is not actually disabled. This is an important change, which should be considered in dealing with any workers' compensation claimant.

"Essential Job Functions"

Assuming an injured worker is "qualified" and "disabled" under the ADA, they still must be able to perform the "essential functions of the job" with or without reasonable accommodation.[14] The term "essential functions" means the fundamental job duties of the employment position the individual with the disability holds or desires.[15]

The initial inquiry into whether a particular job function is essential is whether an employer actually requires all employees in that particular position to perform the function in question. The plaintiffs' inability to meet new speed and quality standards in the case of *Milton v. Scrivner, Inc.*, rendered them unable to perform an essential function of their job.[16] Consequently, their termination based upon their failure to meet these new speed and quality standards was not in violation of the ADA.

Moreover, in the case of *Holbrook v. City of Alpharetta*, the court found that, although a police detective may spend small amounts of time on field work collecting certain types of evidence at a crime scene, collecting evidence is an essential function, which the visually impaired plaintiff in this case could not perform.[17] Consequently, the police detective's termination based upon the fact that he was visually impaired did not violate the ADA, as he was unable to perform the essential functions of his job, with or without reasonable accommodations.

Section 7.4.3

FMLA/Serious Health Condition

The FMLA defines a "serious health condition" as an illness, injury, impairment, or physical or mental condition that involves (a) in-patient care in a hospital, hospice, or residential medical care facility or (b) continuing treatment by a healthcare provider. "Continuing treatment" has been further defined as: (1) a period of incapacity of more than three consecutive calendar days, (2) treatment two or more times by a healthcare provider, or (3) treatment by a healthcare provider on at least one occasion, which results in a regimen of continuing treatment under the supervision of the healthcare provider.[18] Based upon this definition, it is easy to see that almost all workers' compensation injuries resulting in lost time would qualify as a "serious medical condition" under the FMLA. As such, any workers' compensation lost time claim should be analyzed in relation to the employee's entitlement to FMLA leave and the employer's obligation to provide the same.

The Department of Labor published revised regulations effective on January 16, 2009, which changed or clarified several aspects of the FMLA, including the definition of a "serious health condition." The regulations retain the previous definitions of serious health condition, but provide clarification of some of the requirements. One of the definitions of serious health condition clarified when the required "two visits to a health care provider" must occur. Under the new regulations, the two visits must occur within thirty days of the beginning of the period of incapacity, and the first visit to the health care provider must take place within seven days of the first day of incapacity. A second way to satisfy the definition of serious health condition under the current regulations involves more than three consecutive, full calendar days of incapacity, plus a regimen of continuing treatment. The final rule clarifies that the first visit to the healthcare provider must take place within seven days of the first day of incapacity. Thirdly, the revised regulations define "periodic visits" for chronic serious health conditions as at least two visits to a health care provider per year since that provision is also open-ended in the current regulations and potentially subjects employees to more stringent requirements by employers.

Because of the liberal definitions of a "serious health condition," it is possible that an injured worker receiving temporary total disability benefits who is out of work for a period of time, may qualify to take FMLA leave (assuming that the employer is covered by the FMLA and the employee meets the other eligibility requirements). In almost every case, it is to the employer's benefit to run FMLA leave concurrently with the claimant's absence from work. The FMLA regulations specifically state that an employer may require an injured worker who is out on workers' compensation leave to also use his FMLA leave at the same time. In other words, workers' compensation disability time and FMLA time may run concurrently. By taking credit for FMLA leave at the same time as workers' compensation leave, an employer will ensure that it will not be burdened by excessive job-protected lost time due to work-related injuries. However, the employer is also obligated to maintain any and all of the injured employee's pre-existing health benefit coverage, even while he is out on workers' compensation disability leave. The employer would also be required to keep the injured worker's job, or a similar one, available until such time as he exhausts FMLA leave. These legal obligations are not typically imposed by state workers' compensation laws.

Section 7.5

Light-Duty Work as a "Reasonable Accommodation"

As noted above, if a person who is injured on the job is a qualified individual with a disability who can perform the essential functions of the job as outlined under the ADA, and if that individual seeks to return to work, the employer is obligated to go through the "reasonable accommodation" process to determine whether there is light-duty work or some type of accommodation available for the employee so he may return to meaningful employment. Specifically, the ADA's definition of "reasonable accommodation" includes: "job restructuring, part-time or modified work schedules, reassignment to a vacant position, [and] acquisition or modification of equipment or devices."[19] An employer who, as a matter of policy, refuses to provide light-duty work of any kind to a disabled employee who wishes to return to work, may run the risk of liability under the ADA. While the ADA requires that some forms of light-duty work be considered as a "reasonable accommodation," it does not require an employer to create a job that did not previously exist, nor does it require an employer to displace a current employee in favor of the injured worker.

Section 7.5.1

Workers' Compensation – Light-Duty Work

Under workers' compensation laws in most states, there is no obligation placed upon the employer to bring an injured worker back to work in a light-duty capacity. Instead, the only reason an employer may wish to provide an injured worker with light-duty work is simply in an effort to reduce potential liability with regard to the expenses of indemnity benefits. Furthermore, an offer of light-duty work to an injured worker often results in the initiation of settlement negotiations, and eventually brings a long-standing case to a close through settlement. As noted above, however, if an injured worker seeks to return to work, the employer is obligated to go through the "reasonable accommodation process," and may very well be required to provide light-duty work or modified work as mandated by the ADA.

Section 7.5.2

ADA – Reasonable Accommodation and/or Light Duty

The ADA does not require that an employer create a light-duty job for an injured worker. Instead, if an injured employee wishes to return to work, the employer is obligated to determine if a "reasonable accommodation" can be made to allow the disabled employee to return to work. The obligation to provide a reasonable accommodation, however, does not arise until the injured worker requests accommodation. In addition, the employee carries the burden of identifying specific accommodations that he believes can enable him or her to perform the essential functions of the job. In *Willis v. Conopco, Inc.*, 108 F.3d 282 (11th Cir. 1997), the court stated that the ADA does not impose a burden upon the employer to investigate the possibility of accommodations for employees, but it is the employee himself who must come up with some type of suggestion for accommodation.[20]

Courts are split over an employer's obligation to give preferential treatment to a disabled individual for vacant, available positions for which they are otherwise qualified. In *Smith v. Midland Brake, Inc.*, the court rejected the employer's argument that the employee was, at most, only entitled to be considered, along with other qualified applicants, for a vacant position. Instead, the court stated: "[I]f a disabled employee had only a right to require the employer to consider his application for reassignment but had no right to reassignment itself, even if the consideration revealed that the reassignment would be reasonable, then this promise within the ADA would be empty." Other circuit courts, however, have rejected the argument that disabled workers covered by the ADA are entitled to preferential treatment in consideration for other available, open jobs.[21]

On the other hand, an employer's policy of providing only temporary part-time, light-duty jobs was not found to be in violation of the ADA. Specifically, the trial court held that the employer's policy of removing permanently restricted employees from temporary light-duty positions once they were determined to be permanently restricted, did not violate the ADA because "the employer treated all its light-duty jobs as temporary [and, as such] it was not required to make those positions permanent as a reasonable accommodation under the ADA." *Hendricks-Robinson v. Excel Corp.*[22] The case was ultimately appealed to the Seventh Circuit, and the Court of Appeals reversed the trial court's finding of summary judgment, holding that there was an issue of fact regarding whether the jobs offered by this particular employer were really temporary jobs, or in fact, permanent jobs reclassified as temporary.[23] The rule of law, however, remained the same: if the jobs were in fact true temporary positions, the employer had no duty to make them permanent as a reasonable accommodation under the ADA.

Lastly, it has also been determined that indefinite leave requests are not considered reasonable accommodations under the ADA. Specifically, in *Cline v. Home Quality Management, Inc.* (citing *Hilburn v. Murata Elecs. N. Am.*) an employee who was an administrator at an assisted living center was stricken with AIDS.[24] The administrator requested indefinite leave under the ADA as a reasonable accommodation, in hopes that she could eventually return to work in some capacity. The employer did not grant the leave of absence, and instead, terminated her employment. The employee brought an action against the employer for discrimination in violation of the ADA. The court found that the employee's "indefinite leave of absence [was] not a reasonable accommodation under the ADA." As such, the employer's termination was not violative of the ADA.

Recently, however, the EEOC has taken aggressive action against employers whose attendance policies result in the termination of an employee automatically if they are not able to return to work at the expiration of FMLA leave, or after any other predetermined period of absence. The EEOC's position is that employers must consider, on a case-by-case basis, whether some additional leave may be required as a reasonable accommodation for an employee who has been absent from work due to a disability. In some cases, if the employee provides medical certification that he or she may be able to return to work after a relatively brief extended leave, and the requested leave would not impose a hardship on the employer, the additional leave may be required as a reasonable accommodation.

Section 7.5.3

FMLA – Return to Work and/or Light Duty

The FMLA places no obligation on an employer to provide any light-duty work for an injured worker or a worker suffering from a "serious health condition." On the other hand, the FMLA does require that if an employee meets all the preconditions of FMLA leave, the employer may not terminate them for being absent from work for up to twelve weeks. Therefore, an employee who is eligible to take FMLA leave cannot be lawfully required to return to work on a light duty assignment before the FMLA eligibility expires. The employer must also guarantee that the employee is allowed to return to work in his former position or in a position "substantially similar" to his former position when the leave expires. If an individual is not able to return after the twelve weeks of leave, the employer's obligations under the FMLA cease.

Section 7.6
Dual Litigation

In many situations, at the close of a workers' compensation case, when all parties wish to settle the claim in its entirety, they also wish to obtain the employee's resignation and resolve any potential employment claims an employee may have against the employer under the ADA, FMLA, or any other federally mandated statutes. Also, in several workers' compensation cases, an injured worker may simultaneously file an EEOC charge against the employer, alleging an ADA violation. In these situations, the employer is actively involved in defending two concurrent lawsuits. In an effort to resolve all issues at one time, consideration should be given to both the workers' compensation claim and any existing or potential employment claims in any settlement.

Specifically, when the employee agrees to settle a workers' compensation claim, the employer should also request that the employee execute a General Resignation and Release form. In general, this form states that the employee is resigning his employment, waiving his right to pursue any other potential employment actions he may have against the employer, and promising not to reapply for employment with this employer at any time in the future. While this is not an absolute protection for the employer from any potential employment claims, it goes a long way in assisting an employer in defending against any claims that could be filed in the future.

Section 7.7
Conclusion

Following the recent expansions of the ADA and FMLA, it has never been more important to understand the interaction between those laws and applicable workers' compensation laws. It is not unusual for a worker who has suffered a compensable workers' compensation injury to have rights also under the ADA and FMLA, and the unwary employer can easily run afoul of those laws. On the other hand, an employee with a medical issue may have rights under one law but not another. It is possible for a person to be "disabled" or "regarded as disabled" and covered under the ADA, yet not be receiving "continuing medical treatment" sufficient to entitled them to leave under the FMLA. For example, an employee who has been deemed to have permanent work-related restrictions and, as such, is partially disabled from working, but is not under the continuing care of a physician, would likely be covered under the ADA, but not under FMLA. The reverse is also true. Not all "serious medical conditions" under the FMLA are considered "disabilities" for purposes of the ADA. For example, a compensable broken arm, a hernia, or even a back strain—all of which would entitle an employee to workers' compensation benefits and leave under the FMLA—would not be considered a "disability" for ADA purposes. Consequently, when analyzing a workers' compensation claim, close attention must be paid to each individual claim in order to determine which laws interact with the handling of the workers' compensation case at that time.

---

[1] 42 U.S.C. § 12112(A).

[2] *See* 29 C.F.R. § 825.114 (overview of health conditions that entitle an employee to FMLA leave)

[3] 42 U.S.C. § 12112(A).

[4] 42 U.S.C. § 12102(2).

[5] 42 U.S.C. § 12132.

[6] 29 U.S.C. § 2612(A)(1)(d).

[7] O.C.G.A. § 34-9-1(4).

[8] 29 C.F.R. § 1630.2(m).

[9] *Browning v. Liberty Mutual Insurance Co.*, 278 F.3d 1043 (8th Cir. 1999).

[10] *Robertson v. Neuromedical Center*, 161 F.3d 292 (5th Cir. 1998).

[11] 42 U.S.C. § 12102(2); 29 C.F.R. § 1630.2.

[12] *Toyota Motor Manufacturing Kentucky, Inc. v. Williams*, 534 US 184 (2002).

[13] *Sutton v. United Airlines, Inc.*, 1996 US Dist. LEXIS 15106 (D. Colo. 1996).

[14] 42 U.S.C. § 12111(8).

[15] 29 C.F.R. § 1630.2(n).

[16] *Milton v. Scrivner, Inc.*, 53 F.3d 1118 (10th Cir. 1995).

[17] *Holbrook v. City of Alpharetta*, 112 F.3d 1522 (11th Cir. 1997).

[18] *See* 29 C.F.R. § 825.114(a)(2)(i).

[19] 42 U.S.C. § 12111(9)(b).

[20] *Willis v. Conopco, Inc.*, 108 F.3d 282 (11th Cir. 1997)

[21] *See Terrell v. U.S.Air*, 132 F.3d 621 (11th Cir. 1998)

[22] *Hendricks-Robinson v. Excel Corp.*, 972 F.Supp. 464 (C.D. Ia. 1997)

[23] *Hendricks-Robinson v. Excel Corp.*, 154 F.3d 685 (7th Cir. 1998).

[24] *Cline v. Home Quality Management, Inc.*, 2004 US Dist. Lexis 5475 (S.D. Fla.); *Hilburn v. Murata Elecs. N. Am.*, 181 F.3d 1220 (11th Cir. 1999).

Chapter 8
Underwriting

> The ultimate authority must always rest with the individual's own reason and critical analysis.
>
> – Dalai Lama

Section 8.1
Underwriter Insights

As I disclosed in my introduction, I started my career as an underwriter with The Hartford. They had an excellent training program, and the underwriters in our office averaged over twenty years' experience. It was an amazing learning opportunity for me. When I came over to the agency side of the fence thirty years ago, my agency joked that they had to beat the underwriter out of me! The Hartford had apparently left a lasting mark on me! Back then, underwriting was done out of a manual and the underwriters interjected a lot of personal experience and roundtable discussions into their decision making process. They were the epitome of "old school," and used tools and techniques that had been in place for more than fifty years, but times were changing. Computers were just emerging on to the scene and we were witnessing the beginning of computer-generated analytics to help underwriters make better "educated" decisions on which risks they should write and at what price. Since I had a minor in computer science, the underwriting manager kept me close by to help him run reports.

Think about it, thirty-five years ago there were no desktop computers, no automated rating systems, and no fax machines. We had a copy machine, but it was usually out of service. We typically used the old reliable method—carbon paper. That was a time when it took quite a bit of resources for an agency to put together a submission. Since there wasn't e-mail or fax, brokers either mailed the applications to the underwriter or we hand delivered them. Since I was a former underwriter, whenever possible, I liked to hand deliver the applications. This took a lot of time but it gave you a great opportunity to tell your client or prospect's story. This process required you to have both a thorough application *and* a thorough knowledge of the organization, and the two were not synonymous. Back then, every broker could, and often did, complete their own applications. The quality of the submission became a personal trademark of the broker. I give you this brief trip down memory lane because, although underwriters today still want a complete submission, what I see lacking in most submissions now is the thorough knowledge of the organization that was so prevalent in the past.

Consider that most brokers ask for application information, loss runs, maybe your OSHA log, and a brief narrative about your company, which is probably clipped from your website. But I would argue that for an underwriter to give their best pricing, they also need to understand your organization's Safety IQ and Claims IQ, and this is quite often the missing component not being provided by the broker. Additionally, the single biggest change in our business over the past thirty-five years is technology. With technology, the "personal touch" of years ago is missing. The first tip I will give you on underwriting is to ask the broker to give you a copy of the submission they are sending out. While you will want to scan it for accuracy, the real point of this exercise is to ascertain whether your broker is putting your best foot forward in the marketplace. There are a lot of things that should be included in the submission besides application information. Here are a few suggestions:

- An accurate narrative for your organization, including your strategic vision. The underwriter typically will view your website, which is not always an accurate reflection of your organization.

- A narrative outlining your organization's Safety and Claims IQ.

- A copy of the audit your broker has completed on your workplace safety program highlighting strengths and outlining a plan to address the weaknesses. Underwriters love to see this because it tells them that you and the broker are vested in the underwriting process, and the resulting action plans gives them confidence to aggressively price your account.

- A detailed explanation of your claims history. It will take some time for you and your broker to go through each major claim in detail. This will be a great exercise for you, as it will give you some key insights into cost drivers that can be addressed on a go-forward basis, which will help you formulate action plans and performance standards.

- Requests for risk control and claims support. You may find this odd to be part of the underwriting process, but it is a great way to engage the prospective insurance carrier. With so many employers, and brokers, focused solely on price, your broker might actually be able to negotiate a lower cost if he can demonstrate your interest in safety and claims.

Back to technology. You should ask your broker what tool they are using to benchmark your Workers' Comp program. There are many tools available and there is no right or wrong tool. The important thing is that they are benchmarking your program. The reason this is so important is simple—underwriters want file documentation. If you can give them a process improvement plan and periodic updates as proof that you are following the process, they will give you the benefit of pricing based on where your program will be, rather than where your program is today. The key is, of course, stewardship.

Another emerging trend that is going to dominate the underwriter's decision-making is analytics. I am not a big fan of this emerging trend, but insurance carriers are spending millions of dollars, pushed by large analytic consultants, to develop metrics on how to price accounts. This will score and rank risks based on a predictive model that will give the underwriter a very narrow bandwidth to individually underwrite an account. This scares me because the giant analytic companies are triangulating data to decide if you are a good risk based on criteria like class of business, loss ratio, credit score, distance your broker is from your place of business, years in business, size of your company, and location of operations. While I think all of these are important, they are not using any information relating to your Safety and Claims IQ (other than claims) in their pricing model. So, it will mean that you (through your broker) need to work even harder to evidence these programs, since the carrier's focus will rely even more on "artificial intelligence" to make pricing decisions.

Section 8.2
NCCI

In the chapter on loss, under experience rating, we talked about NCCI. If you are in an NCCI state, NCCI often does more than just manage experience ratings. They could file advisor rates, classification rules, and the classification guide.

Section 8.2.1
Classification Rules

One of the publications that most of the industry is familiar with is NCCI's *Basic Manual of Workers' Compensation and Employer's Liability Insurance*. This manual provides the general rules of workers' compensation coverage, classification, premium determination, limits, and special conditions. Each state also has "exceptions" to these general rules. A working knowledge of this reference manual is helpful for anyone involved in the workers' compensation area.

Underwriting

One of the primary subjects of this manual is information regarding proper classification. The object of the classification system is to group employers into homogeneous groups so each group reflects the exposures common to those employers. NCCI uses approximately 600 industry classifications. The experience of each class is tabulated and serves as the basis for a "manual rate." The manual rate is the average rate for all employers in the classification. These industry classes are subject to standard exceptions, general inclusions, and general exclusions.

Section 8.2.2

Governing Classification

Once these exceptions, exclusions, and inclusions have been determined, the governing classification can be selected. This classification most accurately describes the business of the insured and develops the highest payroll. If the class codes do not specifically describe the operation, consider alternative names or synonyms for the industry (Janitor listed as Building-Operation by Contractor or Church listed as Religious Organization). For a business not specifically described in the class codes, use the code that most closely matches its operations. Another NCCI publication, *The Scopes Manual of Basic Classifications*, is extremely useful in establishing the proper class code for a risk. NCCI's customer service department can also help classify troublesome operations. Lastly, a special inspection may be ordered for a separate charge.

There are certain situations where more than one basic classification may be assigned to an individual account. This arises when:

- ☐ The insured's business is described by a basic classification that requires certain operations or employees to be separately rated.

- ☐ The insured engages in construction or an erection operation, farm operations, employee leasing, or operates a mercantile business.

- ☐ The insured operates more than one business in a state. To qualify as operating more than one business, the insured must have a portion of his business as separate undertakings or enterprises (see Rule 1-D-3-c).

Risks involved in construction, employee leasing, farming, mercantile, repair, and recycling operations require further attention.

- ☐ Construction – Class according to each distinct type of construction operations at a job or location. Separate payroll must be maintained.

- Employee leasing – Class as if they are client's employees. Multiple classes may apply.
- Farm operations – Division of payroll allowed for each separate type of farm operation, provided separate payroll records are maintained.
- Mercantile – Class determined by products sold and actual sales. Class also varies if risk is retail or wholesale operation.
- Repair – If there is not a direct class, assign to the product's manufacturing code.
- Recycling – Assign to the closest store or dealer class.

General Inclusions

General inclusions are operations that appear to be separate businesses, but are included within the scope of all basic classifications. Operations are performed by the insured's employees for the insured or the insured's employees, and are classified under the governing class code. The five general inclusions are:

- Commissaries and restaurants
- Manufacture of containers
- Hospital or medical facilities
- Maintenance or repair of the insured's buildings or equipment
- Printing or lithographing

An exception to the general inclusions is when the governing class is a standard exception. In this case, the operations of all employees not included in the standard exception are assigned to the separate basic class that most closely describes their operations. A general inclusion operation must be separately classified if any of the following conditions apply:

- The operation is conducted as a separate and distinct business of the insured (refer to Rule 1-D-3)
- The operation is specifically excluded in the wording of the basic classification
- The principal business is described by a standard exception classification

General Exclusions

The general exclusions are operations of the business that are so unusual that they are excluded from the basic classification. These are operations performed by the insured's employees, used within the business,

Underwriting

and not services to others. They apply even if the governing class includes the "all employees" wording. The five general exclusions are:

- ☐ Aircraft Exposures – These operations are to be separately rated within a 7400 class number
- ☐ New Construction or Alterations – Work on structures owned by the insured and determined by the most appropriate 5000 or 6000 class code number
- ☐ Stevedoring – This includes loading and unloading of vessels and tallying
- ☐ Sawmill Operations – Use code 2710. Includes sawing logs and all incidental operations
- ☐ Employer Run Day Care – Codes 8869

Standard Exceptions E

The standard exceptions are occupations that are common to many businesses. Unless specifically stated in the phraseology of the class code, standard exceptions are rated separately. The exception applies even if the code states All Employees; All Other Employees; All Operations; or All Operations to Completion. The five standard exceptions are:

- ☐ Code 8810 – Clerical
- ☐ Code 8871 – Clerical Telecommuter
- ☐ Code 7380 – Driver
- ☐ Code 8742 – Outside Salespersons
- ☐ Code 8748 – Automobile Salespersons

Clerical Employees are defined as those whose duties include bookkeeping, record keeping, data entry, and telemarketing. Their duties exclude outside sales or any work exposed to the operative hazards of the business. Clerical employees' work area is separated and distinguishable from all other work areas by floors, walls, etc., and does not include inventory areas, product display areas, or sales counters. Clerical Telecommuter applies to an employee performing clerical duties from a residence office that is separate from the employer's location. The Driver's code applies to any employee delivering products owned by the insured, and includes garage employees and employees using bicycles in their operation. The Salespersons exception applies to any employee engaged in duties away from the employer's premises including sales, presentations, speeches, collections, or real estate sales. Salesperson does not include someone who delivers merchandise. The Auto Sales code applies to salespersons on the lots of auto dealers, RV dealers, and boat dealers.

Change in Class Limitations

Changes or corrections in classifications are handled in different ways. Changes in operations are applied pro rata. Corrections that result in a decrease in premium are applied retroactive to the policy inception. Corrections that result in additional premium are handled as follows:

- During the first 120 days of coverage—retroactive to inception
- After 120 but before the last ninety days—pro rata from date of discovery
- During the last ninety days—on renewal

Any misrepresentations or omissions by the insured, broker, or others will apply pro rata from the date upon which it would have applied had the misrepresentation or omission not been made. The reallocation of payroll among classifications, however, is not a change or correction in classification (Georgia is an exception).

Payroll Assignment and Determination

The NCCI has an additional set of rules in the basic manual regarding the proper amount of payroll to apply to the class codes to determine a manual premium. In order to determine proper payroll, the definition of remuneration and its limitations must be reviewed. The basis of payroll is total remuneration (money or substitutes for money). Remuneration includes such items as (complete list in Rule V, B2):

- Wages/salaries
- Total commissions and draws
- Bonuses
- Pay for holidays, sick leave, etc.
- Payments of amount required by law (social security, etc.)
- Allowances for lodging, meals, or other benefits as part of pay package

Remuneration does not include (complete list in Rule V, B3):

- Tips, etc.
- Payment for group insurance or pension plans

Underwriting

- ☐ Dismissal or severance pay
- ☐ Payments for active military duty
- ☐ Expense reimbursement for legitimate business expenses
- ☐ Work uniform allowances
- ☐ Employer provided perquisites like use of car, club membership, etc.
- ☐ Employer contributions to salary saving/retirement plans that are determined by the amount of the employee's contribution

Total payroll is to be included, subject to certain limitations. The first limitation has to do with overtime (pay for hours worked for which there is an increase in the rate of pay). It is the intention of this rule to deduct the amount paid for overtime work in excess of eight hours per day or forty hours per week. Only that portion of overtime payment in excess of the wages, which would have applied if such overtime were paid at the regular rate of pay, are deducted. This limitation applies to overtime, guaranteed wages, and premium pay (night work, holiday, etc.).

Another limitation to payroll applies to executive officers. Executive officers are corporate president, vice president, secretary, treasurer, or any other officer appointed in accordance with the charter or bylaws of the entity. No payroll is included if the officer has no duties and does not come on premises, or the officer ceases to perform duties and does not come on the premises.

Ownership

Since 1990, NCCI rules have provided, with very limited exception, that the experience of an entity continues to be used after a change in ownership. The rules recognize that a change in ownership should not negate the past experience, and that any operational changes made by the new owner will provide an impact solely on a go-forward basis. These rules are intended to provide for the continued use of experience in all cases except where a substantial (material) change is accompanied by both (1) a change in the operations sufficient to result in reclassification of the governing classification and (2) a change in the process and hazard of the operations. If you file for a change in ownership, your broker will help you complete an ERM-14, which is a confidential request for information that is completed by the insured whenever there is a change in name or ownership, merger or consolidation, or when there is common management or ownership with more than one entity.

Classification of Your Risk

You need to pay attention to how your company is classified. Your broker has probably done a mock audit for you in the past to ensure that all of your employees are properly classified. A good rule of thumb is if the premium auditor does not have clarity, they will usually put the payroll in the highest rated classification. One leading consultant on premium audits states that they find errors in 80 percent of the audits performed. Usually these mistakes are in favor of the insurance carrier.[1] I am not saying that they do this intentionally. There is just a lot of pressure to get the audits done quickly, and this leads to error. Your broker can help you by doing some upfront work to help avoid any surprises at audit. We have premium audit tips in the next section.

- ☐ Understand the separation of payroll rule if you have employees doing multiple jobs. This is something that should be done at inception, not audit.

- ☐ Make sure owners', officers', members', partners', and sole proprietor's salaries are capped (if you want to be excluded, make sure the exclusion is filed). If you change insurance carriers, you will have to file a new election form.

- ☐ Make sure you back out overtime.

- ☐ If you don't agree with the audit, many states have an audit appeals board. You do not need an attorney. NCCI states the audit appeal is usually filed with NCCI and they will attempt to resolve the issue. Your broker can tell you if you have an appeals board in your state.

State-Specific Rules

You need to be aware of state-specific rules. Here are some things you should look at:

- ☐ Deductible – You need to know if you are in a net or gross reporting state. In a net state, the deducible (states rules differ on the amount) is subtracted from the claim before it is submitted to the rating bureau. If you are in a net reporting state, you will almost always want to consider taking a deductible. In addition to the premium credit, the deductible will also favorably impact your experience mod. If your broker has ModMaster, they can perform a "what if" calculation to quantify the impact.

- ☐ ERA – If you are in an ERA state, you should carefully monitor your claims. You may want to consider a salary in lieu of comp strategy if you have a claim that will involve a short-term disability. If no indemnity benefits are paid, the claim gets discounted 70 percent when it is reported. Some organizations also require their employees to utilize all of their sick leave before they can draw work comp. If you utilize either of these strategies, be sure to coordinate with your adjuster so they do not issue an indemnity check.

Underwriting

- Classification rules – Most states use the basic rule but you do get some exceptions. For example, in Georgia the reallocation of payroll among classifications on a policy is considered to be a change in classification, and thus, subject to the limitations placed on insurance companies regarding changes of classification.
- Officer, member, partner, or sole proprietor exclusions.

Non-Affiliate Data

PEO, captive, or self-insured groups that do not report their data to NCCI. This varies widely depending on the state that you operate in. You will have to rely on your broker to advise you on this matter. If you want to include non-affiliate data, you will need to complete an ERM-6.

Section 8.3

Premium Audit

You may find it odd that I contain the premium audit section under underwriting. This was not an oversight. I believe premium audits are best handled in the upfront underwriting process. As I previously mentioned, unless you are in the assigned risk plan, the Scopes manual is only a guide for insurance carriers. Unfortunately, brokers sometimes take too much liberty favorably classifying your risk, and you get an unwelcome surprise at audit. There is a tremendous amount of subjectivity in the Scopes manual so you should always discuss your classifications with your broker. You should also inquire about specific classification of individual employees within the class codes on your policy. Let me give you an example with a manufacturing risk. Most of the class codes say if you go into the plant, you fall under the governing code. The Scopes manual is pretty clear on this issue. If you are small facility, the manager is probably out on the plant floor a good bit of the time, but if you are a very large plant, the plant manager probably has more limited duties in the actual plant. Given the great disparity in rate between the governing code (your plant class code) and clerical, this is something that should be fleshed out as part of the underwriting process. Typically, brokers will ask you for payroll broken down by class code and give you a proposal. This process could put you in harm's way when audit time rolls around. Your broker should address any special considerations with the underwriter on the front end, and give you a copy for your files to present to the auditor when they are completing your final (or interim) audit.

Premium auditors work on a tight schedule. Try to have the necessary documentation ready when they arrive including:

- A detailed description of your business operations
- Remember the Scopes manual (NCCI's classification manual) is a guide only (unless you are in the Assigned Risk Plan), and you can negotiate with your carrier if you feel a classification does or doesn't apply. Just be sure and get something in writing.
- Understand the separation of payroll rule if you have employees doing multiple jobs. This is something that should be done at inception, not audit.
- Make sure you back out overtime
- Payroll records
    - Payroll journal and summary
    - Federal tax reports – 941s that cover the audit period
    - State unemployment reports and individual earnings records
    - All overtime payroll breakouts
    - Most payroll systems will allow you to break out the payroll by class code
    - A list of officers, members, partners, or the sole proprietor, and any exclusion forms (make sure they cap payroll if it is applicable in your state)
- Employee records
    - Include a detailed explanation of the job duties of each employee if available
    - Hours, days, and weeks worked annually
- Any cash disbursements or payments
    - Payments to subcontractors
    - Materials
    - Casual labor
- Certificates of insurance
    - Be certain to have certificates of insurance for subcontractors. Many states do not consider independent contractors to be statutory employees; therefore, they are not covered by workers' comp and should not be picked up on audit. Many auditors don't know the difference, and if they don't know the difference you probably will get charged. Not only does this increase your cost, but it also could potentially create coverage when none existed. I had a prospect in Georgia that was a manufacturer. They had a roofer come out and put a new roof on their building. Since the employer was not a contractor, the roofer was an independent contractor not a sub-contractor. The insurer audited the

account and charged them for this exposure because they did not have a certificate. Several months later, the roofer came back to do some warranty work and two roofers fell off the roof. It was as a catastrophic claim and the insurer was estopped from denying the claim because they had (incorrectly) charged a premium. So an incorrect audit could cause higher premiums, but also could potentially open your organization to additional exposure.

- o Have a system to periodically check a sub-contractor's certificate. Most states offer a free coverage verification link on their website. See the employers outline for a link to all the state boards and commissions.

- ☐ Be certain you have documentation about any exceptions that were made between your broker and the underwriter.

- ☐ Meet with the auditor to review the worksheets before he leaves. This is a critical step. If you find that the auditor is not classifying the payroll correctly, try to substantiate why you feel it is incorrect, but do not argue with the auditor. This may result in increased scrutiny of your payroll records, which could lead to more unfavorable results. A better method is to respectfully plead your case, and if the auditor still disagrees, ask him to note your comments in the audit and then contact your broker. Have them fight the battle for you.

- ☐ Ask your broker, before you place your business with a carrier, what their track record is with the carrier's premium audit department.

---

[1] "3 Minute Comp Connections—The Premium Audit," Institute of WorkComp Professionals, website, http://www.workcompprofessionals.com/premiumaudit/.

Chapter 9
Resources

Unless commitment is made, there are only promises and hopes... but no plans.

– Peter Drucker

EMPLOYER RESOURCE MATRIX©

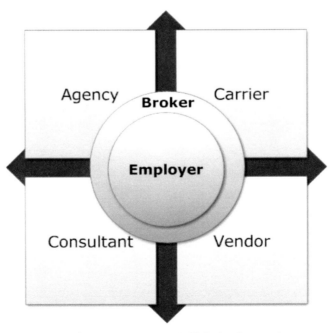

Risk Management Inc. © All Rights Reserved

Resources

Before I begin this chapter, I want to say bigger is not always better. I have always worked in larger agencies that, on paper, have more resource capabilities than smaller agencies. Size may not matter, but experience does! I have seen several smaller agencies that are very adept at outsourcing and are very capable service providers. To help you better understand how to leverage resources to help you reach your objective of an accountable and effective workplace safety program, I developed the Employer Resource Matrix. You will notice in the model I place the broker as the gatekeeper for all of the resources. This is to illustrate the importance of the role they play in helping you achieve your TCOR objective.

Employer

You may find it odd that I start with the employer as the first resource. My philosophy is the employer controls 70 percent of the cost of claims. You do the hiring and firing, and control the safety culture of your organization. The claims adjuster will manage the medical, pay the bills, and send out the indemnity checks, but you cannot expect them to personally connect with your injured employee. If you recall, we discussed this in our chapter on loss. You will be in a position of trust, or mistrust, based on how that employee feels they have been treated up to the time they file the claim, and certainly how they feel after the claim has been filed. So as you look for third party resources, focus on resources that will help you manage the responsibilities that fall on your side of the equation, which controls 70 percent of the cost.

REMEMBER, 70 PERCENT OF THE CLAIMS MANAGEMENT FALLS ON THE EMPLOYER.

Broker

Because a broker is your single greatest resource in controlling your Total Cost of Risk, it is imperative that you place this responsibility in the right hands. The consultative skills of many brokers are really raising the bar for our industry, and with the transparency in the marketplace, the differentiator between brokers becomes their service, also known as their stewardship plan. In having trained hundreds of brokers, I have seen some impressive stewardship plans over the years, but here's the challenge, most brokers are reading from the same consultative handbook, which means they are all starting to sound the same. The titles being used are similar as well. The first time I heard the term "outsourced risk manager" was over thirty years ago. Way back then that was a pretty boutique title. Today that title is commonplace, as is "risk architect" and "risk advisor." Regardless of what a broker calls themselves, there is a lot more that a broker should bring to the table besides the traditional placement of insurance, and you, as an employer, should expect more, so let's discuss how to find the right broker for your organization.

Employers who understand Total Cost of Risk are starting to change the way they bid their insurance program. They are focusing on broker capabilities, rather than the old-school method of letting brokers bid for their business. The reason is simple. If a broker is "capable" of impacting the TCOR, this will have a huge influence on your bottom line. If you agree that insurance costs (premiums and deductibles) are only 20 percent of the Total Cost of Risk, then a 10 percent reduction in premium only equates to a 2 percent reduction in your TCOR. But if your broker can reduce the bigger piece of the pie by 10 percent, that being the 80 percent that makes up your indirect costs, they can show an 8 percent reduction in your bottom line. That number is certainly much more attractive. I recently had a broker tell me "I get paid to sell." I simply asked the question, "Okay, but if you aren't serving as the outsourced risk manager for your client, then who is? And if you aren't, there is a growing list of consultative brokers waiting in the wings to take over your business." It's important to know that while brokers are getting adept at talking TCOR, many fail to provide the tangible processes that will actually impact your TCOR. They can "talk the talk" but is there a thorough understanding of how to exact a plan to impact the 80 percent of the TCOR pie? Which begs the question, why would you bid the smaller piece of the TCOR pie? If you want to have the biggest impact on your bottom line, bid out the capabilities of the broker to help you manage your *overall* Total Cost of Risk.

COMPOINTS

A BROKER MUST HAVE A FINGER ON THE PULSE OF YOUR ORGANIZATION'S SAFETY CULTURE TO MAKE A TRUE IMPACT ON YOUR BOTTOM LINE. TO DO THIS, THEY MUST HAVE BOOTS ON THE GROUND!

But herein lies the challenge—a consultative broker will ask to compete for your business through a capabilities presentation, rather than asking to quote on your business, but with many brokers singing from the same hymn book, how can you differentiate one broker from another? I'll offer several points of guidance for you to consider later in this chapter, but before we get to that, I want to touch upon the importance of the broker/organization *relationship*. You cannot discount this aspect of the service, or stewardship plan, and its impact on your TCOR. I'm very outspoken about my opinion that the risk management process should be broker led. It does not mean that the broker won't have staff involved in the process too, but if they bill themselves as an "outsourced risk manager," they can't pass that title over to their staff. There are so many moving pieces to implementing an accountable and effective workplace safety program, and the broker must have "boots on the ground" to make a meaningful impact. You have to give your broker access to key people within your organization so they can earn a position of trust. That position of trust is essential if they are going to help you make meaningful changes to your safety culture. If this type of broker/organization relationship is in place, it will have a meaningful impact on your TCOR. Conversely, the absence of this relationship will also have an effect on your TCOR—an adverse effect.

I recently conducted a seminar for a large group of employers. I asked them to rank in order of importance why they did business with a particular insurance agency. The broker relationship was overwhelmingly the number one response, followed by the staff, and the agency placed a distant third. I don't discount the power of a great support team behind the broker. In fact, my account executive has been with me for twenty-three years and is a key part of my stewardship plan, as is the rest of my staff. I delegate a lot to my staff, but I am still the gatekeeper of the stewardship plan. Many brokers fail because they want to outsource this entire responsibility. If a broker sells themselves as the outsourced risk manager they should be expected to fulfill that role. More importantly, if a broker lists services in their capabilities presentation, they should be able to give you tangible stewardship examples where the service has impacted their existing clients.

As I said earlier in the book, I am constantly trying new strategies to help my clients, but I disclose that to the prospect or client. I once had a competitor put a great capabilities presentation in front of one of my clients. I admit it was impressive. I knew the broker and knew it was mostly a sales proposal. I told the client to have the broker come meet with him and ask him to write down on a piece of paper his top five clients. The broker complied and listed his top five clients on a piece of paper. After a few questions, my client picked a name off the list and asked the broker to go call his account executive and e-mail him a copy of the last completed stewardship plan. The broker protested and made one excuse after another. My client said the simple question, "If you cannot demonstrate that you have done stewardship on your existing accounts, why should I trust you to complete this plan on my account?" He folded up his notebook and quickly left. This is a fair question, and one you should ask as well.

A good broker will have no problem providing evidence of their track record and commitment to stewardship. When asked for proof, a broker should eagerly want to show you examples of how their service capabilities will help your organization. Trust me, if you ask this one question of a broker, the herd will thin quickly. This question will also demonstrate that you are interested in more than a low price, which will attract consultative brokers.

Below are a couple tips to help you select a consultative broker:

- ☐ Look for a broker that specializes in your industry *or* in a line of coverage that is a cost driver for you. For example, I specialize in workers' compensation, so I help organizations where work comp is their biggest cost driver. The best brokers are typically not generalists; they are specialists. Select a broker who can provide evidence of success in their specialty.

- ☐ Look for a broker who can differentiate your business in the marketplace. How are they going to package your information to create a "feeding frenzy" over your business? For example, when I complete a comP4 audit for a prospect it is a very detailed process that fleshes out the strengths and weaknesses of an organization and generates an objective Workers' Comp Scorecard. We are able to highlight the strengths, and through a series of thoughtful meetings with management, develop a plan to address the weaknesses. This process has a positive influence on the underwriters who price your account. Increasing their confidence in your business leads to more competitive pricing. Select a broker who can outline the audit process they use to help you identify strengths and address weaknesses within your organization.

- Look for a broker who can explain their strategy for targeting a particular market. Their purpose should be for more than just competitive pricing. Select a broker who can demonstrate how they can leverage resources like a dedicated adjuster, customized risk control plan, relationship with premium audit, etc., from a particular carrier.

- Look at the broker's LinkedIn site. This should give you keen insights into the broker's resume.

- Look for a broker who is vested in the process. A consultative broker will be willing to reinvest much of their first year's commission back into your risk management program to build a long-term relationship. Select a broker who will be vested in the process with you.

Agency

Even though the agency finished a distant third in the informal poll I referenced earlier, they still bring a lot of benefit to the client. Rob Ekern, who is a leading TCOR consultant, describes this process as "institutionalization." He defines it as, "the ability of an agency to understand the culture of your firm and you understand the culture of the agency. When this happens it creates a business relationship that transcends the efforts of individuals and creates a business to business relationship." This institutionalization is critical to develop a relationship and trust necessary to positively affect your workplace safety program. While insurance carriers underwrite your account based on your risk characteristics, they also underwrite agencies based on their ability to institutionalize their customers. Simply put, the agencies that can effectively institutionalize a relationship can deliver significantly lower costs.

Below are additional things you should consider:

- Consider small agencies as well as large agencies. I have seen many small agencies that are great in specific niches, so don't discount an agency based on its size.

- Don't eliminate an agency because all their resources aren't "in-house." The use of third party vendors often provides more expertise and is generally more cost-effective. Agencies with "in-house" resources may need to generate fee income to support these fixed costs.

Resources

- ☐ Does the agency "team sell" to bring you a group of experts? Our business is a complicated business and one broker generally cannot be good at everything, so depending on the situation, a "team" can bring more to the table.

- ☐ Does the agency support continuing education? A good agency will have brokers, and their staff, holding specific designations. This commitment to training is a good indicator of the agency's institutionalization.

- ☐ Research the average tenure of the brokers and the staff at the agency. Longevity is a good indicator of the climate and stability of an agency.

- ☐ Look at the agency's website. This can give you great insight into the agency. Using my agency as an example, with a quick scan of our website you would learn that we were voted one of the best places to work by Business Insurance, which means we foster a good work environment. We are part of many professional organizations, which means our agency is vested in our business. We have portal access to many risk management tools, which shows that we invest back in our clients. Our sales team and staff have a lot of designations, which means the firm invests in people. We have a news and issues page, which tells you our brokers do a lot of public speaking. I could go on, but the point is a website can be an easy and informative tool to help you gain insight into an agency. Combine an agency website with a broker's LinkedIn page, and you should have a pretty good feel for the credibility of those you're researching.

Here is a checklist of resources your agency/broker should provide:

- ☐ Mod review and mod trending reports
- ☐ Loss trending on a monthly or quarterly basis
- ☐ Access to a risk management platform
- ☐ A workers' compensation claim professional
- ☐ An online OSHA tool (if you are OSHA regulated)
- ☐ Supervisor training
- ☐ Training material including web-based training libraries
- ☐ A training ROI
- ☐ Set an annual risk plan
- ☐ A annual TCOR worksheet
- ☐ A simple benchmarking process to show improvement

Insurance Carrier/TPA*

The level of service capabilities from insurance carriers vary greatly. Sadly, most brokers don't know how to extract the resources from an insurance carrier to gain traction. Chances are the risk control representative assigned to your account changes at least every couple years; therefore, your broker needs to be the liaison. Below are some things that a risk control representative can provide you:

1. Tap their resources

    I recently had a municipality that was rewriting their standard operating procedures (SOP). I discovered that our insurer had a risk control rep from Mississippi that specialized in writing SOPs, so I arranged to have him fly in and spend the day with my client. It was a mutually beneficial meeting. My client got expert help in developing their new procedures and the insurance company should have a better managed risk due to the strength of the new SOPs. You will be amazed at the resources you can get from your carrier if you know what to ask for!

2. Third party risk control

    If the insurance carrier doesn't have the resources, they may fund a third party consultant. I recently hired an occupational med specialist to help a client develop a physical demand analysis, and the insurance carrier funded the work. Insurance carriers typically allocate 2–3 percent of your premium to risk control, so you should have a say in how the money is spent.

3. Panel counsel services

    If you have a frequency of claims, the insurance carrier may be willing to assign you dedicated counsel, meaning you can affect a relationship with one law firm (note: this will generally be on a state-specific basis). This has a lot of benefits. They will set up a lunch and learn with their panel counsel to discuss proactive legal strategies. They may also be willing to give you a little pro bono work.

4. Information webinars

    Insurance carriers are getting on the webinar bandwagon and some of them can be very informative. Ask your carrier for a list of available webinars.

5. Claims review

    I am not a big fan of claims reviews, but they are necessary. How you conduct them, and how often you conduct them, will be dictated by your number of claims.

---

* Third Party Administrators (TPA) generally only handle claims.

6. Web-based training

   More and more insurance carriers are offering web-based training as part of their service offerings. A learning management system (LMS) is the best way to track your training, but you should definitely check into what types of training your carrier has to offer as well. If they offer free web-based training, most LMS will allow you to track third party training in your LMS.

7. Dedicated adjuster

   It should be your practice to ask for a dedicated adjuster. The insurance carrier may not be able to accommodate your request, but you should always ask.

Consultants

I use a lot of "third party" consultants and vendors. I have strategic partnerships with risk control companies and with specialists, like the occupational med specialist I referred to earlier. I am currently in discussion with a company that develops leadership training, as it's my strong desire to develop a training program for upper management. The use of consultants can bring a very specialized expertise to the situation, as opposed to someone with only a general knowledge of your issue. Be wary of the broker that has all of the resources "in-house." It is a common technique to upsell these services because it is part of the fixed cost of the agency. I suggest you use caution in determining if the "in-house" resources are generalists or specialists. My preference for my clients is to find a consultant that best fits the specific needs of that particular client's situation, and since they are not a part of my overhead, I only bring them in on an "as needed" basis. Should your broker recommend a third party consultant or vendor to you, it is important that you request stewardship examples from their other clients where these services have been used to know if they will be the right fit for your organization. Below are examples of consultants you may want to consider:

1. Nurse triage support

   Company Nurse is a company that helps employers respond to workplace injuries on the "Day of Injury." This is the most critical point at which to influence medical care, claims costs, return to work outcomes, and employee satisfaction. We have a link to a web-based training module for Company Nurse included in our Employer Outline.

2. Actuarial support

   Sigma Actuarial Consulting Group is an actuarial firm that can support larger employer's decision making process on issues like loss pick (to help you decide on your retention level), claim reserve analysis, and cash flow of liabilities. You can download a copy of Sigma's book *Actuarial Advantage* when you register for our Employer Outline.

3. Risk control support

   I have a group of risk control companies I work with depending on the industry type and locations.

4. Physical demands analysis support

   Development of physical demands analysis (www.unicorehealth.com)

Vendors

1. Learning Management System (LMS)

   The LMS tracks user training, and in some instances, it can track live classroom training, and will consolidate all your records in one report. The LMS simplifies tracking, but you don't have to have an LMS to create training. Before you invest in an LMS, you need to do a lot of research to make sure you find one that meets your organization's specific needs. I could not find one that fit my clients' needs, so I had one custom built around my PLOT process. But there are a lot of great off-the-shelf products that may fit your organization's needs, and the good news is the cost of LMSs is coming down.

2. Web-based authoring tools

   If you have an LMS, you may purchase your training from a third party source, but chances are, at some point you will begin developing your own customized training. While the author ware decision is not as critical as the LMS decision, it is still important. The choices vary greatly and most authoring programs offer free trials. Many of the LMS platforms offer author ware with their platform. I use a third party and a built-in tool for my two authoring systems. Even if the LMS you choose has a built in authoring tool, almost every LMS will accommodate a third party authoring tool.

3. Risk management platforms

   I could not find any risk management platforms on the market that met the specific needs of my clients, so I developed the Compass RMS platform. It is a web-based system specifically designed to manage my comP4 Process. I have begun franchising the platform, so ask your current broker if they are a Compass RMS partner. If they are not, chances are they are using the Succeed Risk Management Center or the Clear Risk Platform. Both are good web-based systems that are worth checking out. There are also two good platforms out there designed to manage all of your risk data. On the high end is Origami Risk, and another program, RALLE Warehouse, is offered by Zywave.

If you are evaluating a risk management system here are some questions to ask:

- ☐ Can the workflow be customized around the way you do business?
- ☐ How effectively does the system manage training?
- ☐ Does it include web-based training? If yes, is the training included?
- ☐ What kind of training (documents, video, web-based, webinars, live) does it track?
- ☐ Does it include a safety audit process?
- ☐ Does it include performance reviews?
- ☐ Does it manage a scoring process to assess your risk?
- ☐ Does it integrate with your payroll vendor?
- ☐ Does it track all lines of claims?
- ☐ Does it allow you to track performance standards for claims?
- ☐ Does in integrate claims information with your training information?
- ☐ Does it have a robust reporting system?
- ☐ Ease of use?
- ☐ What is the cost?

If your broker is recommending a risk management platform, please know that all risk management platforms look good in a demo. Ask your broker for references of other clients using the platform. If they cannot give you references, chances are their clients are not utilizing it. Also, the "onboarding" of your data into a risk management platform can be time consuming, and costly to you if you have to pull an employee from their regular duties to manage the onboarding process. I suggest you ask your broker if their agency has an internal onboarding team to assist you with this task.

Risk Management Resources

I have a long list of risk management resources I use. Some are subscription and many are free. If you are an employer and register your book, I will provide a list of helpful resources in the Employer Outline.

Conclusion

By reading this book, you have already evidenced your commitment to improving your workplace safety program. Now you have to put all of this new knowledge into practice. The Employer Outline that you received from my website and the notes that you've taken will help you prioritize your efforts. Making organizational change will take time and resources, so don't lose the inspiration and momentum you've gained from my playbook because you discount those very important facts. Remember, Rome wasn't built in a day, but if you PLOT your course by using the information, methods, techniques, and tips I've provided, you will be well on your way to reaping all the benefits of a safe workplace and a lower total cost of risk. Don't forget to invite your broker to participate in this process. In addition to providing expertise, they can also help you leverage resources from your insurance carrier or TPA. I stand firm in my belief that if you make workplace safety an organizational priority you will get much better traction from your employees, your broker, and your insurance carrier, and you will significantly impact your bottom line.

When we started this adventure, I asked, "If safety is first, then what's second?" Now that you've discovered the secrets of "second," you're really going to enjoy "third"! Stay tuned!

Finally, we all learn by sharing. If you have insights of your own, please share them with us at www.managedcomp.net. I built the CWCP program entirely on word of mouth. If this book helped your organization, please let others know. A satisfied customer is the always the best form of advertisement. And now, my last ask. If I was going to rebrand my safety slogan, what do you think it should be? Let me hear from you.

Thank you for making safety in the workplace a priority for your organization.

Steve

Suggested Reading List

My recommended book list is short and contains books that address some business and personal growth issues. Why is that important? To really make an impact on your organization's workplace safety program, you have to make the message personal to gain traction with your employees. To change culture, you have to first change your perspective, which will in turn enable you to lead change within your organization.

- ☐ *The Noticer* by Andy Andrews
- ☐ *How to Enjoy Your Life and Your Job* by Dale Carnegie
- ☐ *Change the Culture, Change the Game* by Roger Connors and Tom Smith
- ☐ *The 7 Habits of Highly Effective People* by Stephen R. Covey
- ☐ *Carrots and Sticks Don't Work* by Paul L. Marciano

More Resources

Be sure and check out our website at managedcomp.net for some free resources. One resource that you will find particularly helpful is our risk assessment, which evaluates your current safety culture (http://www.managedcomp.net/scoring). In addition to giving you a detailed report, the assessment points you to specific areas of the book that will help your workplace safety efforts.

Another great resource is our Training ROI (Return on Investment) calculator. The calculator was built to help justify the investment in training. If you explore our site, you will see that we are continuously adding new resources.